RICH
INSTINCT

RICH
INSTINCT

THE WORLD IS YOURS
IF YOU CAN SPOT ITS LIES

ALEX CESPEDES

Aktiv Innovations LLC

Dedicated to Cecilia and Ramon,

for giving me all the ingredients

and trusting me to find my own recipe

CONTENTS

INTRODUCTION: WHAT THE RICH AND POWERFUL KNOW

"The greatest trick the Devil ever pulled was convincing the world he didn't exist."

- Keyser Soze in The Usual Suspects

You walk in the room, and the energy shifts. You can't explain it, but you feel eyes on you. Although you haven't said a word yet, you have everyone's attention in the palm of your hand. Some of these people are friends. Some are acquaintances. The rest simply know about you. Beneath the surface, a handful of them are green with envy, but they won't show this. In your face, they'll flash pearly whites, all the while hoping for any opportunity to take what you have.

It won't be today.

Today you're protected by a form of power and intelligence that represents the high point of human potential. Appearances do not fool you. You've internalized at the deepest core of your being that the man-made world around us is based on clever deceptions. You are untouchable for as long as you stay rooted in this feeling. Money, status, health, and influence come to you without much effort.

We've all felt glimpses of this power at some point in our lives or another—whether for an hour, a day, or a year. It's thrilling and addictive. But sadly, for most people on this planet, the feeling is temporary.

Day-to-day, most of us live lives of quiet desperation. We wake up to do work we don't want to do, surrounded by people we don't like, for much less money than we deserve. On top of this, our health keeps declining, and our relationships are strained. Within this lifestyle, the only things that drive us are our obligations—or the thought of the weekend ahead when we can drown out our suffering with our favorite distractions.

Yet, we understand that we wouldn't have to work so hard to stay afloat if we had more money. Without working so hard, we could dedicate more time to exercise and cooking healthier meals. More time and money would also allow us to repair our relationship with our family, friends, and significant other. We can all picture our ideal life, but despite our best efforts, we keep falling short of it.

We fall short not because we're unworthy of abundance but because we've given it away. And we've done so without even realizing it. The world—and other humans—have tricked us into letting it go.

There is, however, one type of person who doesn't fall short. This person is financially independent, so they don't owe anyone an explanation for staying home today. They own their day. They have the luxury of making decisions by Derek Sivers' "hell yeah or no" rule—they do something if it excitingly calls to them, or they decline. They have time to devote to their health, to get the chiseled arms and the six-pack. They have the availability to become leaders in their community. With this abundance of time and money, they can spoil their loved ones as they deserve to be spoiled. This type of person has more than they need. They don't lack anything.

This person who possesses all the above is the *you* that walks into the room and bends the energy of the room. This is the *you* which has harnessed the highest form of human potential. It's the person who maneuvers around the world's deception. This *you* is only different from the mediocre *you* in one fundamental way—a honed intuition against lies. This intuition is how the rich get rich, while lacking it keeps the Masses poor. I call this intuition our Rich Instinct, and our social status hinges on it.

The good news is: there is a simple framework for getting in touch with your Rich Instinct and spotting trickery. Firstly, it requires you to unfollow the crowd because the Masses make choices based on what they see and hear, so they're easily fooled. But the powerful hone their ability to *feel* their way through rugged terrain, thus avoiding traps.

With this upgraded skillset, you'll achieve more influence than you've ever envisioned for yourself. People will pay closer attention to your every word. They will want to help you attain your goals. They will follow your lead. Suddenly, your money pursuits will start to pay more dividends with less effort. And the daily anxiety you experience will virtually melt away. So will those extra pounds around your waist. In short, life becomes the fun adventure it should be.

Throughout history, many have locked in on this state of being and rode it all the way to massive success. Some of these have been towering figures like Warren Buffet, Marcus Aurelius, Cleopatra, and Merryl Streep. They exemplify someone keenly in touch with their Rich Instinct. But for each of these famous examples, there are millions of other superb cases you've never heard of. The abundance and freedom I wish you don't rely on celebrity, name recognition, or flashy money displays. As Morgan Housel wrote, "Wealth is what you don't see." Whether you want to be a household name or just a name in your household, the way is the same.

Following the way makes all the difference.

For decades I've swallowed the sweet lies of the world around me. For decades I've let the world take my best and pay me back with crumbs. Ironically, I'm as ambitious and hard-working as anyone out there. But these qualities alone aren't a proper defense; otherwise, more people would be rich and free. It takes something else to keep your treasure. It takes more to make the world yours.

I recently discovered what it takes.

It takes a specific skill set to become ultra-successful and ultra-free, and it's all contained in your Rich Instinct. I call it an instinct because we're all born with it inside, yet only a few develop it and follow it. But with the right mindset and actions, anyone can grow it to the point it becomes their de-facto decision-making system—a system to dodge lies and acquire life's riches.

This book will show you how to tap into and develop your Rich Instinct. Because this is our only defense against the lies that steal our freedom, time, health, and money. Essentially, it's the key to the world.

I invite you to follow me on this journey as I break down how the world—society, our enemies, and the establishment—throws the proverbial wool over our eyes. If we let the wool remain, we're doomed to stay on the hamster wheel forever. But if we can spot the lies around us, we can keep—and exponentially multiply—our power. With this power intact, our money, health, and freedom will soon grow. Follow me. Let's grow together.

CHAPTER 1:
THE MAN-MADE WORLD IS ALL LIES—AND WHY IT IS THAT WAY

*"The history of all hitherto existing society
is the history of class struggles."*
- Karl Marx

We're all liars. Sometimes by choice, but often from ignorance. It's not a glitch. In fact, the world would implode without lies.

The survival of our species depends on it. Human relationships can only be sustained and nurtured through one form of lying or another. Hard reality to accept, but internalizing it is essential for your success.

We lie every time we respond to the greeting "How are you?" and barely muster enough energy to say "I'm good." Husbands often have to lie when their wife asks how the dress fits. These small lies make everyone's day more pleasant.

And, of course, there are also sinister lies that can cause actual harm. When Bernie Madoff reported off-the-charts returns to defraud customers of $64 billion, he lied. Nixon's lies were his way of stealing the election. Con-men, criminals, and unfaithful partners lie to get what they want. These lies aren't so much a necessity but more of a sad reality of our world. Accepting that there are psychopathic liars out there better prepares us to fend them off.

Now, think about some of the most celebrated individuals in society: Hollywood actors. We idolize Merryl Streep for her ability to fake emotions on command; for her skill at becoming someone she is not. Her lies are part of the show: we welcome them. Deep down, we realize that deception is necessary for survival. We revere actors like Leonardo DiCaprio and Jennifer Lawrence because we wish we were that skilled at hiding our true feelings. If we were as good as them, we think to ourselves, our life wouldn't be so hard. We'd have a much easier time fighting off enemies and thriving.

And some lies actually keep us healthy. Many home remedies have no measurable healing powers; they only work because we *believe* they work. It's the placebo effect. That Vaporub your mom rubbed on your nose and chest didn't help your breathing—science disproved this—but it still made you feel better. The same way a sugar pill can often work as well as Tylenol or Advil.

> *"A world without lies would*
> *be a terrible world.*
> *A world without lies would be*
> *a world without fiction."*
> **- Ricky Gervais**

Lying—like oxygen—is all around us. It is a reality of this world—an inescapable one. So if we can't escape lies—small ones or big ones—the next best course of action is learning to maneuver around them.

That's what this book is about: learning to spot lies so you can keep advancing toward your goals.

Our desires for wealth, love, health, and family are much more attainable than we think—if we wisen up. It's not others' skills at lying that stop us—in fact, most people suck at lying—it's that we foolishly fall for it. It's mostly self-sabotage.

I'm not saying the world isn't dog-eat-dog. Everyone wants to date the popular classmate in high school, while in the professional world, we all want the corner office. Both are desirable *because* they're scarce, so life becomes player versus player.

One day, two friends were walking through the woods when they noticed a bear moving towards them. One of the guys immediately opened his backpack and started to put on a pair of sneakers. The other one looked at him and said: "Are you crazy?! You can't outrun a bear." The first guy responded: "I don't have to outrun the bear; I only have to outrun you."

Life doesn't have to be about competition, but it often feels that way.

Despite our big brains and ability to build nations, humans are still a species within the animal kingdom of Earth. So we're part of the food chain. This chain not only creates hierarchies in tension with all other species but also within each group.

Every pride has an alpha lion who has battled to the top. Humans also battle. Nations used to fight in a field with swords and canons, whereas today's war mainly involves planes and missiles. In our daily life, we can use guns, knives, and fists to fight, but the most common battles today are of wits and words and legal cases.

It's not that we enjoy lying and hurting each other and fighting. It's simply the world we have inherited. The Universe stays in balance through the tension of opposing forces. Light versus dark, sea versus land, noise versus silence. They are locked in a constant push against each other. So it is with humans. Competition in play, work, and sports makes us better. Steel sharpens steel. This tension might hurt us as individuals from time to time, but it benefits The Universe as a whole. Tension is the source of strength.

We generally don't like rain, yet it's needed to grow crops.

We are part of this system. And the highest good we can achieve is to play our unique role to its fullest. As the Army slogan says, "Be all you can be." Only by being our best can we keep the system resilient and healthy.

When seen through this resiliency lens, it's easy to accept that The Universe wants us to be as wealthy as we can be, as healthy as we can be, and as social as we can be. When we thrive as individuals, the Universe also thrives.

Accepting this, it becomes less personal when others lie to us or try to hurt us. We now see it has nothing to do with us; our rivals are just doing their job. The Universe is using them to make us better. Fighting our siblings prepared us to fight the bully at school, and the bully trained us to face jerks at work. They are Non-Playable Characters in the video game of our life.

In turn, they are fighting their own wars, and we're keeping *them* sharp.

> *"Wherever you go you will find*
> *people lying to you,*
> *and as your awareness grows,*
> *you will notice that you also lie to yourself.*
> *Do not expect people to tell you the truth*
> *because they also lie to themselves."*
> **- Don Miguel Ruiz in The Four Agreements**

Most often, when we encounter hostility from others, it's simply that we're in the wrong place at the wrong time. Unknowingly, we just happen to be standing in the way as others move toward their goals. Our choices are clear: move out of their path, fight them, or become collateral damage.

In the old days, others physically cleared people out of their way through fights and wars. Nowadays, people lie. But really, even violent combat has always involved lies. In *The Art of War*, Sun Tzu wrote that all warfare is based on deception.

So you see, deception is the status quo we've been dealt. It was born with The Universe, and it's here to stay. It may not be our fault, but it's our responsibility to defend against it.

We don't have to deceive to succeed, but we must still spot the trickery around us and maneuver accordingly. We get major problems when we're caught unprepared or refuse to move from a position that no longer benefits us.

The primary way others deceive you is by distracting you from reality. They manipulate appearances to make you waste time and energy hitting dead ends. Once you're tired from fruitless journeys, you'll be too weak to fight. The "American

Dream" of consumerism shown on TV is selling you a dead end. Baby Boomers have been the only generation in America that's enjoyed a "middle class" life on a 9-to-5 job which also gave them a comfortable retirement. They benefited from America's powerful position after World War II. And that national prosperity is now gone. Today's reality calls for creativity and hard work, but the TV won't show you that because it's not sexy. It doesn't sell.

Another way others trick you is by giving you things that appear valuable but aren't, hoping you'll give them the precious things they want from you. It's Columbus' men giving Native Americans mirrors in exchange for gold.

Even those with good intentions are playing a deception game. For example, parents have the best intentions when pushing kids to believe in Santa. Within a child, a belief in magic promotes both hope and creativity. Same as when friends cheer on their pal—the aspiring singer—at open mic night, even though his current skills need much improvement. Deception has many uses; it's a Swiss army knife.

Don't blame others for their lies; they're simply playing the game they were born into. The game *we* were all born into. Being mad at the players is a waste of energy. Instead, use that energy to play your best game.

"I was ashamed of myself when I realized
life was a costume party
and I attended with my real face."
-Franz Kafka

CHAPTER 2:
UNFOLLOW THE CROWD: WHY THE MASSES ARE ALWAYS WRONG

The Masses lose because they're always on the wrong side of the cash register. The industrial revolution raised the standard of living for everyone globally, but it did so at a price.

The comforts that have made our life better have also made us dependent. We now want every new gadget or shoe on the market and give most of our income to get them. Meanwhile, the few rich and powerful own the means of production, so they get richer and richer from our spending. As much as possible, your aim should point towards being a producer, not a consumer.

"Wisdom is doing everything
the crowd does not do.
All you do is reverse the
totality of their learning
and you have the heaven
they're looking for...
Wherever the crowd goes,
run in the other direction.
They're always wrong.
Through centuries they're wrong,
and they will always be wrong."
- Charles Bukowski

You don't want to be part of the crowd. You want to be special.

The definition of the word "special" itself provides the blueprint. Things are special when they're scarce, so we value them more. Michael Jordan was special because no one before him could do what he did with a basketball. He was one of one. So if you want to become valuable, you must do uncommon things. You don't have to be the *only* one, but you can't be in the majority. You must do the opposite of what the Masses do.

18

The United States became a world power because it embraced capitalism at all costs. In the nation's early days, the price was tragic and criminal. It enabled slavery, with the comfort of the landowners based on the suffering of many others. Nowadays, slavery doesn't exist, but the economic disparity is bigger than before. The ultra-rich have grown richer, while most Americans are poorer and more in debt than ever.

Studies show 63% of Americans live paycheck to paycheck. The saddest part: a large portion of this group doesn't see anything wrong with their condition. And those running the machine continue to push consumerism. So the lower classes become sacrificial lambs for the sake of the system.

America's laws and monetary system have ended up where a few major players will suck in all the wealth while most others end up broke. Data scientists simulated a betting game where everyone starts with the same amount of money and can bet up to 20% of their total worth at each turn. Each turn is a coin flip, so everyone has a 50% chance of winning each round. You would assume that this 50% chance means in the long term everyone ends up with about the same money they started with. Well, you're mistaken.

What happens is the ones who were lucky enough to win the first couple of rounds start to attract more and more wealth, even if they shortly start losing half of their matches. Since they got an early lead, their 20% bets outpace those who lost their first rounds. Those who lost early on end up playing for pennies each round and can never catch up to the ones who gained the lucky early lead. Welcome to America.

In reality, any slight advantage in the short term gives you a drastically better chance to attract more wealth in the future. It sounds unfair, but it's fair in that the system doesn't dictate the specific *names* of who will get the early advantage, just that money is the lever. It's all about who plays the angles to their advantage first. Given this, each of us should make it our first goal to set ourselves apart from the pack *asap*.

Although the above sounds like an argument against capitalism, it's not. Socialism and other economic systems haven't been able to eliminate the wealth gap either. If there is a solution to this problem, we haven't found it yet.

Throughout history, society has operated on a hierarchy, with a few on top and many on the bottom. Power is distributed this way. So is money. Fame as well. All fields of competition settle into this pattern eventually.

The Rothschild family is worth over $350 billion. Their ascent started in the 1750s, and today many believe they secretly control the banking industry worldwide. If there was ever a true global dynasty, the Rothschilds are it. Many conspiracy theories link the family's power to the Illuminati or to profit from world wars. But the most likely explanation for their longevity is that they were lucky enough to gain an early advantage during the industrial revolution. Like the betting example above, a little bit of money attracted even more money.

As the old axiom goes: much gathers more.

Until humans can figure out how to break this pattern, you and I have only one attractive choice: to join the special few while keeping our morals intact. As the Bible says, "For what will it profit a man if he gains the whole world and loses his own soul?" Corruptness destroys you eventually. But getting to the top by delivering value to others... Now *that* is a worthwhile pursuit. That's what we should aim for.

Your path to the top starts with internalizing Bukowski's advice: wherever the crowd goes, run in the other direction. The crowd is always wrong.

Let's analyze this advice in general terms.

We'll split up the world into two buckets: in one, we'll put the Masses, and in the other, we'll put the Few. Those are two modes of making decisions: you can choose to do the "normal" thing that the Masses are doing, or you can do something "odd." It will vary by situation. Sometimes you'll go with the normal thing, like saying "thank you" when someone holds a door for you. While other times you'll be odd and put pineapple on your pizza.

Different situations speak to different parts of us.

Well, in business, you have more potential customers if you target the "normal" Masses instead of the "odd" Few. It puts the numbers in your favor. Coca-Cola has a bigger market than Aunt Rosie's Loganberry.

But to sell to the "normal" folks, you must offer them something they don't already have. You have to bring something different to the table since the crowd doesn't value one of their own. You have to be—at least in this situation—an outlier.

Outliers are "un-normal." Outliers are, by definition, different from the crowd.

A recent large-scale study by German economists and psychologists identified how the wealthy differ from the general population. One key finding was that the rich are nonconformists. They have no problem going against popular opinion.

Now, does the same work in reverse? If we established that only someone from the Few can sell to the Masses, does the same logic imply that someone normal can find success selling exclusively to the odd folks? The short answer is "no." You can certainly try this reverse approach, but you're starting with the wind in your face. The numbers are working against you since the Few are such minor in number compared to the crowd. And they spend a smaller part of their income on purchases.

Phil Knight, the owner of Nike, becomes a billionaire selling shoes to the Masses. But the owner of the small fruit stand will struggle to sell expensive avocadoes to *only* rich folk. He'll have too much competition for too few customers. To survive, he'll have to either find a competitive edge through heavy investment—which requires him to have lots of money and thus makes him part of the Few—or expand his target market to the Masses.

On the other side of the spectrum, the owners of Louis Vuitton are ultra-rich folks. They sell to rich folk, but some of the Masses also buy their stuff. The flow of money generally only goes in one direction. Up.

Exceptions can and do exist. But break this law at your own risk.

Doing things differently than the Masses—and then selling to them—is the only reliable way to find success.

"When you're on the side of the majority,
it's time to think and reflect on your choices."
- Tony Robbins

Going against the crowd is, of course, the hardest thing to do. It goes against our nature as humans. We're hardwired to be social creatures. Our highest fulfillment and thrills come from our interactions with others. Our species came to rule Earth because we could form tribes bigger than any other animal. In unity there is strength.

In an evolutionary sense, herd mentality is a feature, not a bug.

Think about how things become popular. Hit songs bubble up slowly, but their plays blow up exponentially once they hit #1. The more a song gets played, the more likely it'll keep getting played. The same thing goes for fashion. Vans were mere "skateboarder shoes" for decades, but they blew up overnight when the general public embraced them. They hit what Malcolm Gladwell calls the "Tipping Point." Fads snowball because it seems everyone is doing it. And we don't want to be left behind, so we join the wave too.

It's all a function of mob mentality. We condition ourselves to like things simply because we think our peers like them. Sally likes Levi's because she thinks all her friends like Levi's, and her friends like Levi's because they think Sally likes Levi's. It's our way of feeling "cool" and connected.

"An individual in a crowd is a grain of sand amid other grains of sand, which the wind stirs up at will."
- Gustav Le Bon

Being inside the crowd makes us feel safe. Our closest folks are right there with us, partaking in all the same activities. To leave the group feels like leaving our loved ones behind. The problem is, doing what the crowd does leads to average results. By definition, most people are average. To have what most don't, you must do what most won't. Exceptional results require exceptional behavior. You must make yourself an exception to the norm.

Rainer Maria Rilke said it best, "Again and again in history, some people wake up. They have no ground in the crowd and move to broader, deeper laws. They carry strange customs with them and demand room for bold and audacious action. The future speaks ruthlessly through them. They change the world."

If taking the road less traveled seems like too big a price to pay for success, this confirms you *really* need a change of course. It means you've drunk the Kool-Aid. You have given up independent thought for the comfort of the crowd. Create some distance to reveal the behaviors holding you back. You need space to see the bigger picture.

"To understand one's world,
one must sometimes turn away from it."
- Albert Camus

This bigger picture reveals defective systems that promote blind obedience and restraint. For example: schools.

Schooling Is Broken

Formal education has not lived up to its promise. It started with good intentions of equipping everyone with necessary skills but has now been corrupted by self-preservation. Somewhere along the line, school transformed into a mechanism for creating obedient workers.

To be fair, school is great for teaching children how to socialize. And it keeps them occupied while their parents work. It also teaches fundamental math, reading, and writing skills efficiently, which are all positives.

But past age 13, schools become less about learning and more about showing off for fancy colleges. At 13 years old, kids stop asking, "Why?" and start asking, "Is this gonna be on the test?"

Past 12 or 13 years old, students' priority shifts towards getting into the best high school, so they can get into the best college and after graduation get the analyst job at McKinsey or Goldman Sachs. School has become a brainy pageant where the prize is servitude. Or, as Pink Floyd famously sang, "just another brick in the wall."

I understand professions like medicine, law, and engineering can't exist without traditional higher education. Outside of these though, the usefulness of adolescent schooling drops rapidly.

You don't need traditional schooling to learn skills. The fancy terminology and the degrees often get in the way of real learning. Skills are a hands-on process. Michelangelo didn't go to art school, and you can figure it out too. The Universe can be your teacher.

I've now worked in corporate America for over a decade. And I see how school groomed us to be obedient cogs in an assembly line. It beat out of us any questioning of authority. We're programmed to please our boss—who in turn only cares about pleasing *their* boss. This programming starts at school, where they teach us to feel at home in the crowd. And to desire only what the Masses desire.

I wish I had a solution to the school problem, but I don't.

To offer some background: from a young age, I hated writing. No one explained why I had to write about the symbolism of Holden Caulfield's name. They just said, "Do it or fail." So I begrudgingly complied. It was a chore, not an act of creativity.

Now I write for fun because I see the value of crisp communication. Writing well can get you paid, laid, and saved. It's a powerful skill when done with passion. And torture when done without it. If school hadn't forced writing down my throat, I would've loved it much sooner.

School is how they inject into us the virus of conformity. It teaches us how to color, but only within their lines. The "best" student is simply the best rule-follower. They don't tell you that those who live best make their own rules.

Unsurprisingly, many of today's richest tech founders are college dropouts. Facebook's Mark Zuckerberg is the most obvious example, but the list also includes Steve Jobs, Michael Dell, Bill Gates, Larry Ellison, Jack Dorsey, Daniel Ek, and so on. They are out-of-the-box thinkers, and school was holding them back. The colleges they dropped out of are now their customers.

You and I are made of the same stuff as Michael Dell and Jack Dorsey. If we re-ignite our independent thinking, we can also create enormous value for society. And we can also attain the riches that come with it. But we won't get there following the crowd. We won't get there painting within established lines.

Not only does school limit our independent thinking, but it also keeps us down financially too. Noam Chomsky explains, "Students who acquire large debts putting themselves through school are unlikely to think about changing society. When you trap people in a system of debt, they can't afford the time to think. Tuition fee increases are a disciplinary technique, and by the time students graduate, they are not only loaded with debt, but have also internalized the disciplinarian culture. This makes them efficient components of the consumer economy."

To be clear, there is no coordinated school conspiracy being planned in a dark basement somewhere. And most teachers are generous folk with genuine intentions. If they could change the system, they would. But the machine is too big to steer. It has gotten this way through a natural progression of events across generations.

The push for schooling comes first from our parents as they were pushed by theirs.

Parents are too busy working to see the side effects of schooling. After getting home from a 10-hour work day, all a tired parent desires is a child who will stay put and follow orders. Unconsciously, our school system becomes an extension of their effort to raise a child that's obedient at home.

Once engrained, however, the submissive behavior doesn't stay at home or school. In the real world, those who look to exploit us are good at pushing the obedience buttons created by schools. If enemies know they can get away with controlling us, they'll gladly do so.

So if you're not where you want to be, just know there is a whole system nudging you along with the current. Peer pressure from the crowd and the school system pushes you to fit in. But at any point, you can choose freedom.

Ultimately, you can train yourself to spot the lies that hold you back.

Our Mind Is Complicit in the Trickery

Given that anyone can become a good lie detector, why are the Masses still living under deceit?

There is an excellent explanation for this.

The Masses live under perpetual deceit because the human mind *prefers* lies. Early trauma from our childhood leads us to believe life is dangerous and hurtful. This plants a desire for anything that numbs our pain. Even if they're fiction and completely bad for us, most folks prefer pretty lies over unpleasant truths. We are so thirsty for relief that we *want* to believe life is rosy when it isn't.

Pretty lies release dopamine in our brains. It's our brain's "happy juice" and makes us feel great. In this way, fantasies recruit our biology as a partner in crime. Our whole being's momentum pushes us toward pretty lies. Is it any surprise, then, that liars never lack an audience of eager ears? We'll almost always choose the dopamine rush of a desirable lie over the downer of an undesirable truth.

Think back to your own life. Haven't you found yourself in relationships where your partner promises the world while slowly ruining your life?

Haven't you heard things like "I'll change," "I would do anything to make you smile," or "I would never even look at someone that isn't you?" All the while, things just get worse.

Haven't we all been at jobs where the boss tells us, "You are going to reach the top of this company quickly," or "Your value to this firm is priceless," only to be overlooked come promotion time?

When you hear any of the phrases above, run the other way.

They're red flags that you've stuck around too long. Time to bounce.

But we hardly ever do. Because the sweetness of those words is much more desirable than the facts: that we're heading down a dead end.

But only the truth shall set us free.

Only reality can make us independent thinkers.

At our core, every one of us feels that we are being deceived. We also feel that life isn't black and white, but instead, a shade of gray that requires we live in the gray too. Yet we ignore the feeling out of convenience.

Most of our anxiety comes from that cognitive dissonance in our gut and head. Things aren't matching up. Parents, schools, and religion preach honesty and obedience. But deep down, we know there are times to disobey—or lie—to survive. Baltasar Gracian said, "We get three educations in life. One from our parents, another from school, and a third from the world. The third one contradicts everything we learned from the first two."

CHAPTER 3:
THE KEY: DON'T TRUST YOUR EYES OR EARS— INSTEAD FEEL YOUR WAY AROUND

The Few—the small portion of the population with riches and power—don't hold a "secret formula" for success. All humans—rich and poor—internalize the ingredients to success as children. We all know that prosperity comes to those who bring value to the world. And that getting there requires work and collaboration. Bill Gates is a billionaire because Microsoft provides value for companies and individuals. Their tools help people get organized.

No secret formula there.

But this is where things get interesting.

Those in power use the same formula as everyone else. But their power comes from plugging different *variables* into that formula.

For example, algebra taught us about the linear equation $y=mx+b$. But the answer for "y" depends on the numbers you plug in for the variables m, x, and b. Someone who plugs in 3, 5, and 8 will get the answer $y=23$. While someone who fills in 4, 6, and 9 will get $y=33$. *This* is where the Few are different. They live their life choosing the *right* inputs. It's almost like they see the world through a different lens. But they're simply more closely connected to reality, while a veil of illusions obstructs the Masses.

The Few experience life differently than the Masses, so their formulas are filled in with more accurate data.

To become rich and free—to live a better life—you must make decisions based purely on the best information. And the best information is available to anyone determined to find it.

To properly explain how this works, we must first take a step back. More specifically, we need to step back in time... 2,400 years.

In his piece, *The Republic*, the ancient Greek philosopher Plato told The Allegory of The Cave. The allegory serves as a powerful metaphor. In the story, he describes a group of people who, from a young age, have lived deep inside a cave. They live chained up, facing a blank wall.

On a higher plane of the cave live a second group of people, unchained. They use objects to project images onto the blank wall that the prisoners face. Think of them as Puppeteers. The objects, shaped to resemble real-life things like cows and trees, are put in front of a fire. The light of the fire creates the shadows that the first group sees on the wall.

The chained prisoners look at the projections on the wall in amazement and terror. They hear the voices of the Puppeteers and think these sounds are coming from the projected shadows. Since they've lived inside this cave for as long as they can remember, these projections are the only world the prisoners know. They give names to these images and develop stories to explain the shadows.

Plato argues that most of society is like the first group chained at the bottom of the cave. They can't remember the natural world outside the cave, so their emotions are controlled by fake projections of objects on a wall.

According to Plato, the Puppeteers represent society's major institutions, like the government, schools, and artists. The Puppeteers attempt to show the prisoners fragments of the world through the projections. Still, ultimately these are mere images that perpetuate the status quo of society.

There exists, however, a third group. These are the philosophers who, through their efforts, have been able to break free from the chains of the first group and climb up to escape the cave. These free persons now see the sun and all the natural things found outdoors. They see real cows and real trees now, not the shadows of figurines.

Plato tells us that only a small number of prisoners break free of their chains. Some of them will encounter the Puppeteers and decide to join them, while a smaller number will keep climbing out of the cave to see the sun and the real world.

If some of this sounds familiar to you, you're onto something. Plato's Allegory of The Cave inspired the Wachowskis as they wrote The Matrix movies. Great art always contains ancient wisdom.

How the Rich and Powerful Experience the World

With The Cave, Plato was trying to give us a blueprint for leveling up our life. He understood that the Few who possess riches and power take in the world differently than the Masses, thus getting better results.

We've established that humans are prone to lie out of habit, even when their intentions are pure. The allegory above explains some of this: we don't know any better. How can one speak the truth if one hasn't seen reality? We're stuck in the cave, so we can only speak of the projections we see, not reality itself. We lie without realizing we're lying.

Similarly, our governments, schools, and industries are showing us the world as they think it should be, not as it is.

And we continue to fall for it.

The Masses only know life in the Cave, so everything they communicate to each other is based on these fake projections as the starting point. They don't understand that what they see and hear isn't trustworthy.

But the Few gain—and retain—power because they don't trust their eyes or ears. They understand that anything around us that's man-made is society's projection of the world, not the world itself.

The Few avoid the reasoning and story-making of the prisoners, who try to explain what they see. Instead, the Few have grasped that understanding reality is impossible; one can only *feel* it.

To succeed, you must develop the gut-based compass that the ultra-successful live by. This compass is your Rich Instinct and your only guide in a world that can't be understood. So don't try to understand it. Feel it.

The Answer Has Been in Front of Us All Along

The concept of feeling your way around—instead of using your eyes and ears—is a squishy subject. What does "just feel it" even mean?

Here is where your other senses come in, metaphorically speaking.

Some ancient cultures revere the Third Eye. It's said to be located around the middle of the forehead and represents enlightenment or higher consciousness. The Third Eye has no solid scientific basis, but the concept is sage. Our standard eyes aren't the most reliable source of information from the external world since that's how society tries to fool us. Alternatively, the Third Eye collects vibrations and chakras only a person primed to receive them can perceive.

Like Spider-Man has his "spidey sense," which flares up when danger's near, so is your Rich Instinct a robust tool for avoiding lies. It's the equivalent of a superpower. A superpower that shows you the way to a better life. Our Rich Instinct is the key to a world of riches, health, and freedom.

In concrete terms, feeling your way around is about ignoring what a situation *appears* to be and learning its real nature through hands-on experience. It's less about observing and more about acting, followed by re-acting. It's about trial and error, and the power of iteration. It's the difference between watching an instructional video on riding a bike and learning by physically riding one.

The Masses are so busy being terrified by the perception of what they see—and the fears society instills in them—that they take no action, or weak action, towards their goals.

The Masses spend years discussing their new restaurant idea, always waiting for the "perfect time" to start. The Few spend four weekends building a food cart to pilot at their neighborhood Little League games, then adjusting their plan or scaling up.

The Masses wait for January 1st to roll around and start their two-a-day gym sessions, only to give up by January 15th. The Few start with ten pushups today and increase them by one daily. Fast-forward ten months, and they're doing 300+ pushups daily with a chiseled body as proof of their consistency.

The Few know that the toughest obstacles are invisible before you start. Only by taking steps towards your goal do you learn of the hurdles. And only then can you work to overcome them. So why wait?! Start now. The real solutions will never make sense in advance; otherwise, the problem would've already been solved. We can conquer a problem only by gaining a feel for it from the inside, where few dare venture.

This advice has been told to us for ages, but its simplicity has kept it hidden in plain sight.

The Bible gave us scriptures that read, "Walk by faith and not by sight" and "Take the first step even if you can't see the whole staircase." It's the concept of *feeling* in action. You can't see the whole staircase since man-made illusions hide it from you. But when you take that first step, you feel the Universe supporting you. Rumi, the poet from 800 years ago, taught something similar when he wrote, "As you start to walk on the way, the way appears."

You won't see the way in advance; you can only feel it as you walk.

Socrates hinted at something similar thousands of years ago when he said, "I know that I know nothing." He grasped that the world is far more complex than we assume. When you think you've figured it out, you get blindsided by a new type of trickery. Yet, despite claiming not to know anything, the Socratic method he invented uses repeated probing to bring us progressively closer to knowledge. It's a form of feeling your way through, even if just conversationally.

In The Bible, we also find Proverbs 3:5, which reads, "Trust in the Lord with all your heart and lean not on your own understanding. In all your ways acknowledge him, and he will make your paths straight." Even if you don't believe in God or a specific religion, we can all agree that there is a form of energy inside all matter. Energy that makes plants

43

grow, and humans reproduce. This force can be called "reality," which operates by the laws of physics. Human hands can't taint reality; instead, it rules over all man-made creations. With that in mind, reread the scripture and substitute "The Lord" with the word "reality." This is what you get:

"Trust in reality with all your heart,
and lean not on your own understanding.
In all your ways acknowledge it,
and it will make your paths straight."

Don't try to understand it.
Feel it.
What you see is fake.
What you feel is real.

Most people stay at the bottom of the cave because they focus on what they see and hear. So they're scared by the stories playing out on the walls. It's not the chains that keep them down, since these are easy to break with some movement. It's really just fear that keeps them frozen in place. But if they would start feeling around with their hands, wandering and bumping into walls, then adjusting, and feeling where the draft of wind is coming from,

44

they'd be able to find their way up the cave. They'd start leveling up and eventually escape to the outside.

It's dark in the cave, but darkness is also part of life. It's good for you. It forces you to develop courage and faith—the drivers of new value in this world.

Wallace Wattles advised that getting rich is simply about doing things in a "certain way." In one regard, this means there is a specific, repeatable set of steps that will get you to the level of wealth others have achieved. In another respect, he's telling us that taking these steps with certainty—another word for faith—is necessary for success. Weak action brings weak results. If you're going to do something, do it boldly.

In a modern example, the legendary writer Ray Bradbury left us with these words:

"Don't think. Thinking is the enemy of creativity. It's self-conscious, and anything self-conscious is lousy. You can't try to do things. You simply must do things."

"Feeling your way through" means turning the volume down on the man-made data in front of you and focusing on the experience as a whole. It's a visceral ordeal. An instinct. A Rich Instinct.

Your eyes and ears are how others will try to deceive you, so don't trust what you see or what others say. Think of your eyes and ears as spies working for the enemy. If you follow them, they'll lead you off a cliff.

Puppeteers are only concerned with keeping the convenient status quo since it keeps them in power. And they succeed for a while. But life is change. Life isn't stillness with a bit of movement mixed in; instead, it's mostly motion with brief periods of perceived calm. It's because we've ignored our Third Eye that we don't sense the chaos of the Universe.

It's the reason why most humans lie—even the sincere ones. A human mind is too small to comprehend the vast mysteries of the world, so most of us can't consciously distinguish fact from fiction. Hence why the best method is to feel around and flow from experience.

In the 1970s, Dr. John Diamond worked in behavioral kinesiology. This field starts with the belief that every stimulus an individual experiences will make them stronger or weaker. Dr. Diamond developed procedures that tested the effects of certain stimuli on a patient's muscles, showing them what could make them ill or cure them. He outlined these in his book *Your Body Doesn't Lie*, setting off an entire movement.

Another doctor, David R. Hawkins, took this further by asking his patients specific yes or no questions, then testing their physical balance. He found that a person's balance felt firmer when their words were in sync with absolute reality. Meanwhile, even when they weren't consciously aware of a lie, their body became less stable.

The reality is: our gut knows more than we do. We run into problems when we ignore it, falling for appearances or overthinking. As Malcolm Gladwell wrote in his book Blink, "We need to respect the fact that it is possible to know without knowing why we know and accept that sometimes we're better off that way."

Have you ever met someone and disliked them immediately? They didn't say anything to offend you, and you have no prior information about them. Yet you can't shake the feeling of disgust. You still give them the benefit of the doubt, only to later learn your first impression was correct. This is your gut showing its power. Something tripped the alarms, but your brain pressed the override button.

The fundamental nature of things and situations is moving too quickly for any human's consciousness. You can't reason your way closer to reality; you can only feel your way toward it.

The word "truth" is subjective, so I don't like it. I prefer the term "reality." Because the truth can be manipulated, but reality can't. Truth is just a word; reality is a feeling.

We have two brains: our primitive mammal brain—the inner core—and our outer, more-developed human brain capable of language and story-making. Our mammal brain provides our "gut instincts," the feelings we can't explain. In contrast, our developed outer cortex is the part that processes language and seeks to find rationality, making it the portion of our brain that can fall for lies or fantasies. But our unconscious brain isn't weighed down by language, allowing it to process its surroundings faster. Our mammal brain is too busy keeping us alive to care for promises, making it a more reliable source for decision-making.

Let's rely more on our mammal brain while training our outer brain to spot the signs of manipulation. If you can do this, life becomes fun. It becomes an adventure. A game to be enjoyed and played masterfully.

Your Weapon Against Appearances

So now we've internalized that appearances will lead us astray. But can we do anything to build up our defenses when the visual, man-made world is flooding our eyeballs?

Yes. The remedy is The Neutralizing Question.

The Neutralizing Question is simple, and you should ask yourself this question throughout the day before making decisions.

Warning: the answers will sometimes scare you.

Pause for a moment, and ask yourself this:

"What choice would I make right now if I assumed what I see and hear is all false?"

I know the question sounds cynical, but don't worry. It's designed to re-frame your thinking. If you are excited, this question dampens the adrenaline so you're not swept in by it. And if you were feeling fearful prior, the question provides hope that there are more options on the horizon. This calms your nerves so you can regain your balance.

It's not about rationalizing since rationalizing leads us further from reality. It's about turning the volume down on your thoughts and turning the volume up on your instinct. Your gut knows what's too good to be true. Your gut also knows how resilient you are when faced with adversity. Trust it. Let it talk to you.

You'll notice that pausing for this simple question makes you feel more connected to the reality of the situation. Remember, even those with good intentions sometimes give out false information since all they see are projections on a wall. And those with bad intentions are used to getting their way quickly, so even a moment's deliberation on your part now pushes them back on their heels.

You think you're doing better financially because you have a bigger house, a nicer car, and expensive clothes. But what does your bank account tell you at the end of the year? Is your net worth higher than at the beginning of the year?

You think you're moving up in your career because you have the fancy VP title and the corner office. But do you have greater control of your time? How much influence do you have towards making things better? Often the reality is the opposite of what we see.

When you eat certain foods, you think you're eating healthy. But how do you feel an hour later? That's the accurate barometer of healthy eating.

Like all of life's best strategies, this approach is simple but not easy. In the beginning it will be quite difficult, but stick with it and you'll experience life-changing results. You have to ignore what you see and go with what you feel. For example, someone who flashes their wealth often doesn't have any (or doesn't have as much as you think). They're showing fake idols to distract you from their real intentions. If it were football, they're pulling the equivalent of a flea flicker: they pretend to run but pass the ball.

Taking a moment to question your eyes and ears grounds you. Your balanced stance will cause you to feel calmer and more empowered. Now you're ready to experiment and maneuver your way forward.

"Re-examine all that you have been told...
Dismiss that which hurts your soul."
- Walt Whitman

The Scientific Method

On your road to a better life, it also helps to become a lie scientist.

In the same way scientists are rigorous with their theories, so should you be with your beliefs. Write down everything you believe to be true and real. Now, try to find all evidence that negates it. Force yourself to take the opposite side of the belief, like a prosecutor trying to prove a defendant guilty. If you put in enough effort, you'll notice at times, your opinions start to slip. Doubt creeps in. This is great for showing your brain's susceptibility to persuasive messaging. The mind is indeed a sponge that absorbs both poison and panacea. It doesn't discriminate.

Other times you'll find that after attacking your beliefs, some of them don't waiver. Instead, they become more deeply rooted in their absoluteness. These are your pillars of reality and are what will guide you to success and riches.

Maneuvering to Success

The world is a chaotic place by nature. The lies of our manufactured society only make it more chaotic and mysterious. We must instead gain a feel for reality.

You gain a feel for things only through hands-on experimentation. Through trial and error.

If you are scared of trial and error—or are easily shamed—remember that no one is born fearless. Fearlessness must be developed like a muscle.

If you're hoping to avoid the anguish of hands-on learning, then give up hope for any success. Success and safety cannot coexist.

Success requires, above all, massive courage.

Only massive courage will allow you to walk by faith and not by sight. Because, remember, our eyes and ears are working against us. They're being flooded with fake information by others. Most of what you see is an illusion. Machiavelli wrote, "The great majority of mankind are satisfied with appearances, as though they were realities, and are often more influenced by the things that seem than by those that are."

The Masses are swayed by appearances, so they are doomed to stay in the cave. The enlightened Few have a pulse on reality and move accordingly. Learn to distrust appearances. Learn to feel your way through.

CHAPTER 4:
THE ROADBLOCK TO EVERYTHING YOU DESIRE: THE FOG

If you pay close attention, you'll notice lies all around you. Deception is such a devastating force that it has penetrated every area of our lives. It's on your screens, in your conversations, in the food you eat, and in the things you buy. Like a Trojan horse, you let it into your life, and then it kills you.

You know that feeling first thing in the morning? You're half awake but kind of half asleep too. It's not just groggy. You get out of bed, and your balance is off. You can't even tell what's real and what isn't. I compare the deception around us to this feeling because it forms a barrier between you and the real world. I refer to society's systemic deception as "fog." It makes your mind foggy.

Fog is any object, food, story, drug, promise, vice, or lie that distracts you from seeing what's really going on around you.

And only once identified can you reduce, eliminate, or protect yourself from its claws.

A prime example is television. TV is a wide-reaching form of fog that sweeps all corners of society. In America, it's a major tool used to control the Masses since, as a country, we watch too much TV.

What—or whom—you allow to steal your time and focus, becomes your master. In this way, much of the population is a slave to screens.

Reality shows, sitcoms, music videos, infomercials—they all show us aspirational lifestyles that don't exist. We might know this, but it still impairs us because our brain *wants* to believe in it. Life seems tough enough; what harm is there in a bit of escape?

A lot.

TV fogs up our brains and leaves us open to deception.

Even if you know it's fake, the poison of watching TV comes from the commercials built in—and around—the content. Every few minutes, they try to sell you something else you don't need. They're pushing on you a way of life that is both unaffordable and unhealthy. Everything you buy opens you up for another related purchase to fit your upgraded lifestyle. It's a slippery slope into consumer slavery.

How can you ever hope to gain control over your life if you spend every dollar as soon as it's earned? The lower and middle classes don't move up because of their spending habits.

Beware of free content. Mckenzie Wark put it this way: "If you are getting your media for free, this usually means that you are the product. If the information is not being sold to you, then it is you who are being sold."

Your eyeballs, personal information, and viewing patterns are being sold to multinational corporations. Armed with this knowledge, they can develop even better ways to sell you more stuff.

But the most poisonous of all TV is the news. The news doesn't make money from informing you; they make money from keeping you tuned in so they can show you more commercials. To do this, they feed on your fear and curiosity. They manipulate every story into a real-life horror movie, making monsters out of mere mortals. The news channels pick a side, then turn the other side into "evil villains." Real-world issues are rarely clear-cut, but the news makes them black-and-white, throwing out reality in the process. Avoid the news at all costs.

> *"Television is by nature the dominator*
> *drug par excellence.*
> *Control of content, uniformity of content,*
> *repeatability of content make it*
> *inevitably a tool of coercion,*
> *brainwashing, and manipulation."*
> **- Terence McKenna**

Another enemy to consider is food, specifically junk food. Food is for nourishment, but industrialism has weaponized it. Big companies push on us so many delicious options that we've lost our ability to feel satisfied. We can't stop ourselves from overeating. Overeating—as well as eating the wrong things—keeps our brains foggy and dependent. When we're overstimulated by food, our capacity for decision-making drops. Then we become easy to deceive.

Fog short-circuits our willpower and discipline.

Anything you use as a crutch is a form of fog. Drugs, alcohol, nicotine, those delicious Haribo gummy bears, TV, porn, and social media—all of these allow you to escape problems for a moment. But once their effect wears off, you're lower than before. They are poison disguised as a time-out.

Now consider how many of the above forms of fog the average person consumes daily. Add to this the gradual comedown period they exhibit, and it's not a stretch to say the Masses live their entire life fogged up. That perpetual state of being under the influence, I call it "the Fog." The Masses *live* in the Fog.

The Fog

The Fog is the persistent system of vices that keeps us from seeing the world as it is, making it easy for others to exploit us.

On its own, a vice like TV doesn't seem harmful. The same goes for junk food. Even alcoholism is often swept under the rug. As a kid, heavy-drinking adults would get a pass as merely "bohemian" or "a liver of life." We all learned to let alcohol abuse slide. And so it became the big, swollen-faced elephant in the room.

In poor neighborhoods, it's almost a given that every adult will medicate the hardships of life in one way or another. Everyone drinks, smokes, snorts, injects, gambles, or eats their miseries away.

Add on top the TV binging and the credit card debt of the lower/middle classes, and you have a powerful web of addictions that keeps the Masses trapped for life.

All the vices above steal one's freedom of thought, action, and time. Not to mention how they weaken one's financial standing. These vices collectively drain one's power and re-distribute it to the suppliers. In this way, the customer is *never* right.

It's a hard pill to swallow, but most of us currently live in the Fog. I'm fighting to get out, and so should you. While we might not fit the clinical definition of an addict, we're addicted to the *combined* effect of all forms of fog we take in. We've been in the Fog so long that we don't even notice it's there.

The Fog is so sinister because it masquerades as reality. Upon closer inspection, though, it has its own color and texture, like an alternate reality. In Indian culture they call this alternate world "Maya." They liken it to a "magic show, an illusion where things appear to be present but are not what they seem."

Fog Adds Unnatural Hue to Your Life

Reality has a whole different hue than life in the Fog. Reality is gray, never black or white. In the real world, nothing's entirely "bad" or "good," always a bit of both. A failure in business is never fully a bust. Like Edison said, "I have not failed 10,000 times— I've successfully found 10,000 ways that will not work."

A setback is merely a setup for a comeback.

Reality's grayness means there's a certain stability to life outside the Fog. When stable, we can focus on finding the positive angle to every situation and discard what doesn't serve us. We develop incredible resiliency.

Inside the Fog, life consists of extremes. It seems rigidly divided into either work or play—time to be serious or time to celebrate. During "playtime," things are seemingly bright and sunny since we drink, eat, and party. Alcohol, junk food, and drugs are specifically engineered to bring one up and provide moments of ecstasy. This makes the Masses forego restraint and spend chunks of their paycheck—or worse, max out credit cards—for a mere few hours of enjoyment.

Whole industries exist just to siphon off savings from the Masses and funnel them back to business owners. Think about the nightlife industry and the luxury goods industry. I've known folks who worked full-time at a pharmacy making $600 a week, then watched them spend $300 for their outfit plus $300 for a bottle on Saturday night.

I've pulled similar stunts, racking up $1,000 credit card charges to spend a night beyond the velvet rope.

YOLO. You only live once, right? Well, working 40 hours for a paycheck and then spending it all in one night is not what I call a life.

How can one hope to gain financial freedom with this kind of math? It's impossible. Which is why many are doomed to stay in the Fog forever.

Taking in fog keeps us enslaved until we break the cycle. Alcohol, TV, junk food, and drugs; all of these make our world look sunny. And when we feel great, we're likely to spend more. The more we spend, the deeper the hole we dig for ourselves, and the more depressed we feel. Then, craving relief, what do you think we run to? You guessed it: the alcohol, TV, junk food, and drugs that put us in this mess to begin with.

We also get the other extreme climate inside the Fog: catastrophic storms. Work seems like cruel and unusual punishment instead of what it should be: a chance to find meaning by serving others. Or an opportunity to at least earn financial freedom.

The Fog is full of imaginary storms. News and crime documentaries give us the impression of danger around every corner. The media industry follows the motto, "If it bleeds, it leads." The most violent and gory events get top billing. Our fear is now piqued, and we stay tuned in, allowing the channels to make more money by selling more commercials. William Randolph Hearst built his fortune on pushing panic. Fear is an effective form of control.

The Fog around us vacillates between extremes. At one moment, life appears to be all sunshine and rainbows, while the next moment, it is full of violence, storms, and crime. Given this, is it any surprise that the Masses drug themselves to celebrate, then fall low and use those same substances to medicate?

The Few who live outside the Fog know to avoid things that paint life in extremes. Outside the Fog, you can prevent extreme emotions since your attention goes to the things you can control and nothing else. When you step off the rollercoaster of the Fog you have more control over your journey.

The comforting news is—it's all a choice. Each one of us, if we want it enough, has the option to step off the rollercoaster and escape the Fog.

Three Groups of People—Which Type Are You?

In 1911 at age 30, the painter Pablo Picasso finally achieved financial stability to match his fame. He moved from a cramped space into a large apartment with a built-in studio located in the classy Paris neighborhood of Montparnasse. With this new living and working arrangement he could work undisturbed as long as he liked—and his art got even better. He would wake up late, then head into the studio from early afternoon until the evening, when he would invite friends over for drinks and partying. Once the entertaining ended, he'd feel a rush of creativity and often return to his studio, where he worked late. He thrived with this new freedom to live as he saw fit. By all measures, Picasso now lived outside the Fog.

I believe the purest form of success anyone can attain is living on their terms. Someone who wakes up every day at the time they choose to wake up, to do the things they choose to do, surrounded by the people they have chosen to be with—to me, that person is a living symbol of success.

Picasso is a famous example of someone who lived on their own terms. But it's the thousands of unknown winners that should appeal to you most. Those are the ones who have the most flexibility to do what they want whenever they want with whomever they want. They live unbothered.

Although this model of success sounds simple on the surface, beneath lay many moving parts. Living life on your terms, by definition, requires that you have financial freedom, mental freedom, and time freedom. In essence, that your decisions aren't forced upon you by circumstances. But the road that leads you there is only apparent to someone who sees the world exactly as it is. It requires the clearheadedness of someone firmly rooted in reality, not someone enslaved by the Fog.

Therefore, you will only find true success outside the Fog.

Inside the Fog, we work 40 to 80 hours a week just to survive. Outside the Fog, we work not because we need to but because it's how we fill our lives with meaning. Through service to others, we also serve ourselves. Work is a beautiful thing when it is work that aligns with our natural talents and makes life better for others. But when work reduces our financial, mental, or time freedom, it no longer serves us. At that point, it's bringing us deeper into the Fog.

Inside the Fog, we live our lives based on what neighbors, family, friends, or the news tell us to do. Outside the Fog, we live by what we feel is right for the growth of ourselves and our community. We are on a sure-fire path to misery when we fall victim to mob mentality and propaganda.

Inside the Fog, we live for the weekend since our jobs own our weekdays. Outside the Fog, we live every moment as we choose because we own our time. When we own our time, we are free to pursue the activities that fulfill us and provide value to our close ones.

Outside the Fog, the essential things get done without hurry or worry. We are fully engaged in the moment at every moment and thus able to express every function God intended for us.

To live outside the Fog, an individual must have financial, mental, and time freedom. Anyone missing one or more of these isn't fully outside the Fog. They could be close to the outside but not fully out. Essentially, there are levels to this.

We've been calling those living outside the Fog the "Few," and those currently living deep inside will be called the "Masses." But there's also a third group. We'll call those who are inside the Fog yet trying to escape "Insurgents" because they're rebelling against the status quo of their current world. Being an Insurgent is not about a specific position in society; it's more about a direction and speed of travel. I am currently an Insurgent, and if you're reading this to learn how to escape, so are you.

My wish is that everyone joins the Few since living outside the Fog is the only way to fully express all our talents. The sad reality, though, is that not everyone will make it out. Leaving the Fog requires extraordinary actions—and by definition—rejecting the ordinary pleasures of the crowd. Although you can have allies in this great escape, it is, first of all, an internal struggle—and therefore an individual journey. You must make peace with the fact that others can only escape at their own pace, if at all.

The deciding factor in this journey has nothing to do with race, gender, religion, or education. The deciding factor is simply courage. Do you have the courage to make the tough choices needed to escape? That's the ultimate factor.

Given that courage is the deciding factor, one would assume that the Few have much more courage than the Masses or Insurgents, but that's not the case. The Few only needed enough courage to take the first step. Because after the first leap of faith, they get a taste of life on the other side. And it thrusts them forward. They learn to trust their feeling over their fear. We can never internalize this concept if we never take our first leap. A movie scene I'll never forget is Indiana Jones taking that first step onto the invisible bridge in The Last Crusade. It made all the following steps much easier for him.

**

So how many people live outside the Fog? There is no way to know precisely, but for illustrative purposes, we'll say at any given time, 5% of the population lives outside the Fog while 95% are inside.

Why choose arbitrary numbers like 5% and 95%? Well, in competitive environments—like academics, sports, or finances—you'd have to fall in the top 5% to be considered truly special. This number applies in cultural arenas too. For example, the Black Muslim movement calls their leading thinkers "Five Percenters."

We've also stated that financial freedom is essential to being part of the Few. Well, if you look at household net worth in the US, the top 5% are the ones who can live comfortably off their investment income alone. They don't need to hold a job or liquidate assets to maintain their lifestyle. Granted, not everyone who is financially free also has mental and time freedom, so our numbers shrink a bit. On the other hand, some talented folks can produce passive income without a high net worth, so our number expands again. This brings the estimate back to 5%.

The Groups Are Fluid

Remember that 95% and 5% are back-of-envelope numbers for illustration. The more significant point is both groups are constantly in flux. Some of the Few will regress back into the Masses, and some Insurgents from the Masses will make it outside and join the Few. Although earlier we said that the powerful seem to always stay in power, this is only what *seems* to be. Some powerful Few are sliding into the Fog daily due to carelessness or unlucky tragedy. There is always some degree of change in the ranks. Life is change, and through this change nature stays in balance.

Insurgents like you and I are the keepers of nature's balance. We've woken up to how the world works. We reject fantasy land. We've noticed there is no single villain with a master plan to deceive us.

Instead, we've learned the system is made up of many independent entities working towards self-preservation. We now understand that the best defense against the system's oppression is to get as close to reality as possible. Only by being rooted in reality can we protect our financial, mental, and time freedom.

All of the above changes are happening daily, so we should not be discouraged by thinking it's too late for us. It is never too late to change your station in life. This book you are reading is the first of many positive steps for gaining more power and freedom, no matter where you currently stand.

"Let me tell you why you are here.
You have come because
you know something.
What you know you can't explain,
but you feel it.
You've felt it your whole life,
felt that something is wrong with the world.
You don't know what,
but it's there like a splinter in your mind,
driving you mad.
It is this feeling that brought you to me."
- Morpheus to Neo in The Matrix

CHAPTER 5:
GAINING MENTAL AND
FINANCIAL FREEDOM

On most days, I'm the model of a productive person. I wake up early, go to the gym, work efficiently, spend time with my loved ones, and go to bed at a decent time. But when I drink heavily, alcohol turns me into a person I call "Rico." Rico is usually the center of the party—dancing, talking loud, eating anything he can find, and encouraging others to follow suit. Sometimes Rico appears after four drinks, other times after seven of them, and some days it takes 10+ drinks to summon him. He's a wildcard.

I know one thing about Rico though: when he appears, I won't be productive again for at least 30 hours. The day after drinking heavily, I can't get myself to work, can't get myself to focus. All responsibility goes out the window. It brings me down low and crushes any momentum I have. For this reason, I now try to limit myself to two drinks max per day. Fun is fun, until it isn't.

Moderation Is the First Step Towards Freedom and Power

The first step to escaping the Fog of lies is moderation. There is nothing wrong with indulging in junk food from time to time. And it's understandable that once in a while you'll binge on a TV show you like. The same way it's OK to enjoy drinks with friends on occasion. The key is understanding that these substances add unnatural color to how you see the world and diminish your grasp of reality.

When you're drinking alcohol, everything seems more emotional and dramatic. When you're on caffeine, everything seems more interesting. One bite of junk food makes you crave the next bite more, and the one after that even more still. Soon you're bloated and sick. All forms of fog cloud your judgment and promote poor behavior in the moment. But the higher the high, the lower you'll go during the hangover. In the process, you've wasted valuable money, time, and energy.

The vices coming at you are many, but the technique for fighting them off is always the same. You must create some space between you and temptation. This space buys you valuable seconds to weigh the incoming temptation against your life priorities. Every time you say yes to something, you're saying no to something else.

Economists talk about opportunity cost. The opportunity cost of doing or buying one thing is the value of the best option you leave behind.

Let's say you have two job offers, one that pays $30 per hour and another that pays $40 per hour. If you choose the one paying $40, your opportunity cost is the $30 job you said no to. If you go with the $30 job, your opportunity cost is $40. Your best option always has the lowest opportunity cost.

If you spend $100 on a pair of shoes, that's $100 you could've invested in the stock market to multiply on its own. Life is about choice. And when it comes to buying things, our choices can make us prosper or go broke.

Deep down, we all intuit society's hypocrisy. We feel the pressure to say "yes" to nice things, knowing full well those things enslave us. Yet, without some of these desirable objects, we can't attract the support we need to escape the Fog. So it puts us in a Catch-22. We believe our only choice is to play with fire, hoping to do so without getting burned. "If I get the big house and car," we tell ourselves, "this will put me in a class of people that can help me make more money." Sadly, the ego boost of having nice things is the most addictive drug of all. In trying to be the deceivers, we lose our footing and fall for the deception ourselves.

It takes constant effort and self-control to keep our minds clear of the fog of vanity. Just because society gives status to those with nice things doesn't mean it's the only way to gain status. Choose games that give you the best chance of success. Most status games are essentially Ponzi schemes in which you're already late and become someone else's stepping stone in the pyramid.

Moderation requires a bit of willpower. That's the price of admission to the outside: a bit of suffering to protect your priorities. That little bit of suffering, of self-denial, brings you closer to reality. It clears your vision in the Fog. You become grounded in reality through sacrifice. We should all aim for this goal: to be far from fabrication and fully immersed in reality. This is true freedom.

"There is no higher rule than
that over oneself,
over one's impulses:
there is the triumph of free will."
- Baltasar Gracian

Mental Freedom

Living outside the Fog isn't a place or a permanent destination but a manner of living. You could be part of the Few and standing next to someone fully immersed in the Fog. Your spouse could be in the Fog of vices and drugs while you're safely outside its clutches (although this is a rare combination). Your next-door neighbor with the fancy house could also be living in the Fog. The point is that although financial freedom is a big part of leaving the Fog, you won't be free until your inner self is free.

James Clear said, "Power is influence over external events. Peace is influence over internal events." To gain mental freedom from the Fog, you must have some inner peace and clarity. It keeps you free from the vices of the Masses. You must hone your radar to spot the lies of society and others. This requires daily work because slipping back into mental dependence is so easy.

"The best drug is a clear head."
- Harald Juhnke

One of our biggest assets is our attention and focus. Once someone or something has your attention, they know they've got you. Where attention goes, energy flows. So don't give fog your attention. Focus instead on your own goals, on your own life, and you won't be tempted to look at the flashy spectacles of the Fog. Minding your own business is a superpower.

Those who don't have much going on for themselves will be the ones who spend all day gossiping. Those are the critics who find a fault in everything the doers do.

That's why the news is so toxic. It steals your attention with gore, drama, and violence. It hooks you, then fills you with so much fear that you never dare create anything of your own. Instead, it pushes you to buy useless products that help you "cope" with your fears and to work your whole life for someone else's company at a low but "secure" wage. It turns you into just another critic; it kills your inner creator.

Fear and elation are two sides of the same deception coin. Being too high up is just as bad as being too far down. Both keep your mind dependent and unfree.

Gaining Financial Freedom

Whoever said "money can't buy happiness" didn't have any. To be fair, love and health rank higher than money. But although money can't guarantee you'll have love or health, being broke will surely push the other two away. Those two things require time, which enough money can free up for you. You see, money is not material; it is spiritual. It is a measure of how much you're serving those around you. It can buy you material things if you choose to spend it that way, but the most important thing money gets you is freedom.

If you're struggling to make the end of your money meet the end of the month, you are a slave to hustling for a buck. You can't have mental peace if you're constantly worrying about rent or food money. Even if your financial situation isn't so bleak, I bet you still do many things you wouldn't choose to do for free. You're putting up with nasty co-workers, carpooling with neighbors you don't like, and doing work that goes against your core values. Those all demand your time and energy, restrict your freedom, and lower your defenses against the Fog.

To break free of the Fog where the Masses live, you need space between yourself and financial troubles. You need time to come up with subtle maneuvers. Both of these require money.

The dilemma here is that *money isn't real.* It looks real and sounds real, but it's not real. Things are real. Value is real. Exchange is real. But money in and of itself is simply a story taking place within the Fog. Governments worldwide print money and inject it into the black hole that we call the economy. They have to do this because it's the only way to keep the Masses working since those in power don't like to do menial work.

Like all facades, there's no guarantee this scheme will be sustainable forever. So their plan is to inject money into the system while the Masses still respect it, and while everyone's distracted working, they purchase assets that can outlive the scam. Since they're the ones printing the money, the Puppeteers can choose which areas and industries the money flows to, as if they could tell clouds which city they want it to rain over. With this knowledge, they go in and buy the city before it rains money over it, leaving the rest of the country feeling like a desert. That's where the Masses live—the desert.

As someone looking to escape the Fog, our job is to find the chosen "city" and claim some of it before it rains. Only this way can we catch some buckets of money rain and gain our freedom.

This is all a long way to say: I understand why you want money. Even though it's not real, you want money because the Masses believe in it. They will give up their time and their life for it; they'll do what you want for something that isn't real. Working for something that isn't real is tragic, but *you've* been doing the same all your life in the Fog. Unless we're born into a rich family, we all have to pay our dues for a bit. Fine. But it's now time to escape.

If you want freedom, you need lots of this fake thing called money.

Will and Ariel Durant studied the entire history of human civilization to identify patterns. One of their most important findings was that "the men who can manage men manage the men who can manage only things, and the men who can manage money manage all." Money trumps both physical skills and management skills. If you have enough money, you can hire for any skill you don't have. Money is leverage, and leverage is power.

To gain personal power you *need* money.

Understand: your wealth is not about reaching a set figure; your wealth is a ratio between your income and your expenses. It does you no good to earn ten million dollars a year if your expenses are also ten million dollars. That's a ratio of 1 to 1, so any hiccups in your cash flow could mean bankruptcy. But if you earn one million dollars a year and only spend a hundred thousand, your ratio is 10 to 1— meaning you are wealthy.

For many, a 10 to 1 ratio sounds like an impossible dream, but I urge you to get as close to 10 as you can. It is possible.

The first step to wealth is finding ways to keep more of the money that comes in. This doesn't mean becoming a penny pincher—quite the opposite. Most people underspend on things that could make a difference in their lives while overspending on the wrong things.

The right things to spend money on are those that multiply on their own, while the wrong things deplete and drain growth.

Spending generously on healthy food amplifies your vitality and energy. Therefore it's a great investment that adds value to your life. Whole foods are typically more expensive than processed foods. Still, they satisfy you for longer, helping you avoid overeating—and thus—obesity as well. Whole foods also keep your head clear, allowing you to make better decisions at work and at home.

For driven folks, spending on a business is also a wise use of funds. Owning a business multiplies your leverage and power. The thing about business is that it's capital-intensive. It takes money to make money. To thrive, you'll likely have to raise capital from outside investors, or you'll have to borrow some. Either option works. The point is that pouring into a business is a positive step towards bringing abundance to yourself and those you serve.

Other things that multiply on their own: stocks and real estate investments. If approached with patience, owning stocks and real estate can make you rich over the long term. They're not for day trading or "get rich quick" strategies since this is high risk and akin to gambling. The purpose of these investments is to lock away your money and "plant seeds" that could grow immensely years down the line. Nassim Nicholas Taleb recommends a "barbell" strategy where most of your investments are ultra-safe, while a small part goes into high-risk investments that could yield 10x or 100x returns. Notice what you're doing here: you're moving away from the "middle" where the Masses play. The Masses are always wrong.

The blueprint is clear: it's possible to become rich while having a job, but it's not wages that will make you rich. You get rich from profits, not wages. It's the money from wages you save—to then funnel into *investments*—that will make you rich. The profits from those investments are what can make you rich. A job is merely an intermediate step to investing in profit-producing assets. Business owners and money handlers simply bypass that middle step since all their energy goes directly into the investment part. Entrepreneurship is a lot riskier, but when it works, it's a quicker way of getting rich.

Just remember, everyone's path to wealth is unique. There are countless ways to get rich. You have to find your own special recipe that fits your personality.

Another great way to spend your money: skills. If a skill will help you level up your career or business, spend on it. This doesn't mean degrees or master's diplomas. As mentioned earlier, student loan debt is one of the worst kinds of debt. Good investments are books and reasonably-priced equipment that could expand your money-making opportunities. Workshops, software, and personal tutoring; these are other seeds that could grow into money trees down the line. However, most often, the best investments come in the form of time. Time invested into focused skill-building is never wasted. I've learned it always proves useful down the line.

Spending on cultivating relationships is also a great place for your funds. Aid to someone who needs and deserves it will always come back multiplied, even if through other avenues. Like skills, though, the best and most common way to invest in these is simply with your time. Be careful not to be someone who "buys" their friendships. Giving the right way—to worthy members of your tribe—multiplies itself in the long run. But giving indiscriminately to everyone around you is a recipe for ruin.

Understand: the amount of money you earn isn't dependent on how much you work; instead, it depends on your leverage. The word leverage comes from "lever," a thing that can move something bigger. The stronger your lever, the bigger the stuff you can move. A skill can be a lever. Connections can be a lever. Political votes can be a lever. Assets can be a lever. Your goal is to build a lever that others need and will rent from you for a price.

The wrong things to spend on are the ones that quickly make you broke. Buying a bigger home than you need is like asking for trouble. A bigger space begs to be filled with more things you don't need. Things that drain your bank account and decrease your ratio of income to expenses. It also invites unwanted visitors that bring drama into your sanctuary. Freeloaders love vacant rooms like a fat kid loves cake.

"Keeping up with the Joneses" is a well-known yet overlooked expression in America. As Morgan Housel wrote, "Spending money to show people how much money you have is the fastest way to have less money."

Some more expenses that shrink your life and freedom:

- New cars: unless you have a good business reason to buy a new car, buy a three-year-old used car instead . You'll save 50% of the money and won't think twice about loaning it to friends, thus creating more good Karma.

- Outlandish weddings and birthday parties: these fall in the same category as keeping up with the Joneses. They're about flaunting your status in front of people who aren't even that impressed anyways.

- Fashion: personal appearance is very important. But you have to be brutally honest with yourself before buying wearables. Ask yourself if you're falling victim to vanity or if this is absolutely an investment that could pay off.

- Tourist travel: I'm all for learning about new places and cultures, but most trips aren't about this for Americans. Instead, most people travel to show off to their peers. They want to take cute photos at the same places their friends have also taken photos at. Others vacation hoping to escape the inner work they should be doing instead. But it's inescapable. As John Kabat-Zihn says, "Everywhere you go, there you are."

The items in the list above are both roots and symptoms of *lifestyle inflation*. One bad decision begets another bad decision. Like bricks, they pile up until you're a prisoner of your own jail.

Remember, the Masses are always wrong, so you must do the opposite. When times are good, most people increase their spending because they have a surplus. And when times are tough, the Masses start cutting back on spending. You must reverse this. The Universe works in tides, so when you catch a large wave, that's your chance to build up reserves. Cut back spending while things are good.

And when times look bleak, you should spend some of your reserves since they'll have a bigger impact than usual. Good stock investors know that fortunes are made by buying at the bottom of bear markets; you just need patience. If you cut back during lean times, you're promoting a feeling of scarcity within yourself. Those around you sense your panic and retreat from you. You dry up your attraction of abundance.

Warren Buffet has a powerful contrarian tactic. He says you should "be fearful when others are greedy and greedy when others are fearful."

When times are tough, you must find self-multiplying areas to spend your money on. You have to shake things up and get abundance back on your side. When others feel scared is usually the best opportunity to buy assets at a discount. Invest heavily in your business or career during dry times; your money stretches further than usual in fire sales. It's also a great time to become the new leader of the pack. Recessions show up when the old way of life is no longer working, so fresh ideas are needed from a fresh face.

You must cultivate the correct philosophy of money so that wise decisions become automatic. This takes courage, though, since it will earn you many critics. These critics are very often the people you love most. It's OK to be misunderstood because inside, you know you're doing it for them. They might ridicule you for not splurging on lavish parties or vacations, but when emergencies show up, they'll be glad you have reserves to help them out with.

There will come a time to spend lavishly on things and parties, but they're only justified when they stop breaking your bank account. First, you must focus on becoming financially independent, and that requires some sacrifice in the short term.

"Saving is the gap between
your ego and your income."
- Morgan Housel

Being financially independent and escaping the oppression of the Fog is the noblest thing a person can do for their family and community. Wallace Wattles wrote about this beautifully in his book The Science of Getting Rich:

"Whatever he can say, no man can be really happy or satisfied unless his body is living fully in every function, and unless the same is true of his mind and his soul. Wherever there is unexpressed possibility, or function not performed, there is unsatisfied desire. Desire is possibility seeking expression, or function seeking performance.

Man cannot live fully in body without good food, comfortable clothing, and warm shelter; and without freedom from excessive toil. Rest and recreation are also necessary to his physical life.

He cannot live fully in mind without books and time to study them, without opportunity for travel and observation, or without intellectual companionship.

To live fully in mind he must have intellectual recreations, and must surround himself with all the objects of art and beauty he is capable of using and appreciating.

To live fully in soul, man must have love, and love is denied expression by poverty.

A man's highest happiness is found in the bestowal of benefits on those he loves; love finds its most natural and spontaneous expression in giving. The man who has nothing to give cannot fill his place as a husband or father, as a citizen, or as a man. It is in the use of material things that a man finds full life for his body, develops his mind, and unfolds his

91

soul. It is therefore of supreme importance to him that he should be rich."

As Mr. Wattles wrote above: we cannot live fully without freedom from excessive toil. It is one of the biggest roadblocks to getting out of the Fog. Humans were made to work, but not excessively so. Too much work puts you on the hamster wheel that many call "the rat race." The rat race means we're hooked on consumerism and fall into the vicious cycle of wanting more. Soon the things we own end up owning us, as this lifestyle requires we stay in the race. We'll be stuck in subpar pursuits unless we have some freedom to leave the rat race and look around.

When your employers want to keep you under their control, they pile work on top of you. They give you more things to do than you can handle. They know you won't get to it all, but you'll do some of it. And more importantly, you'll be so stressed that you lose the capacity to defend yourself. You stop questioning why you're working so hard and they aren't. You become a mindless robot, a task rabbit. You lose your ambition to work towards true power.

*"When you redefine the pursuit of wealth
as the pursuit of freedom,
you give yourself permission
to authentically want it.
It's no longer a dirty wish."*
- Thomas Waschenfelder

To cultivate our innate talents, we need free time to work on them. You must work harder on yourself than you do for others. Don't spend all your energy at your job and not put the same effort into your own ambitions. The Masses are the ones who work only when they get paid, the rest of their time being spent on mindless pleasure. But Insurgents and the Few put in work towards improving themselves. You'll find that the tasks you would do for free are the things that end up paying you the most down the line. These are the activities you put your whole self and soul into, the things you're likely to stick to because they fulfill you without external rewards.

You want to be a producer, not a consumer. To be rich, you must get on the other side of the cash register—the side where money comes in, not out.

Those who get rich achieve it by doing things in a certain way. By certain, I mean with a high degree of willpower behind it, as in, with *certainty* that you will succeed. There's a word for this; it's called faith. Only by doing things with faith, by acting despite your fears and doubts, will you provide other humans with what they most need and desire: hope. Giving hope to your community is the highest-value activity one can perform.

Since The Universe is seeking to expand at all times, it can only do so by pushing against the resistance of entropy. Therefore all the organisms inside the Universe must push for more life. Pushing requires the fuel of hope. When you do things with faith, you provide hope. And hope expands the Universe for all. For this, you'll be rewarded with more money than you'll ever need.

CHAPTER 6:
FUEL UP YOUR LIFE FOR FREEDOM

Money tends to give people amnesia. Once they're rich, they forget how much of a struggle it was to get there. I'm working my way out of the Fog, so I'm the perfect person to tell you how it is on the front lines.

Gaining financial, mental, and physical freedom in this deceptive world feels that way: like a war. One where the battles are taking place on multiple fronts. Your mind, body, and finances are under attack at all times. Think of Napoleon fighting against the Anglo-Portuguese army on one side of the continent and the Russians on another.

Taking any other approach but 100% dedication to this war—is a recipe for failure.

But there's good news: by simply reading this book, you're already better equipped than someone doing it alone. The seeds of thought in these words have already ignited your inner transformation. What follows are some tools and tips to help you develop a Rich Instinct and escape the Fog. Also ahead, some hurdles you can expect to encounter.

Health Is Your Fuel

Good health is both an aid and a benefit of leaving the Fog. While in the Fog, our health is under attack because oppressing the mind also hurts the body. To free your mind, you must free your body too, and improving your health is an investment in your freedom.

Regarding nutrition, scientific studies are constantly contradicting each other. Be skeptical of everything. Large food companies can sway doctors and scientists. But one guideline has stood the test of time: whole, natural foods are superior to anything processed. Ask yourself, did God make it look like this, or did man do it? The closer it is to its original form, the better it is for you.

The problem with processed foods is that they create inflammation inside your body. These foods strain your organs as they try to repair the damage. This is why you often feel bloated and sluggish after eating the wrong things. Sugar, flour, dairy, processed vegetable oils, and alcohol give you a momentary high. Soon though, your mind gets foggy from the toxins attacking your system. Modern living makes it tough to *completely* eliminate toxins from your diet, but the less you consume, the lighter you will feel.

"No drugs or alcohol so
I can get the signal clear as day."
- Andre 3000 of Outkast
in the song "ATLiens"

Remember, you can't go by what you see or hear. This is how they trick you. You have to go by how food makes you *feel.* **That's your barometer for healthy choices**.

Wait an hour or two after you've eaten, then ask yourself: "How do I feel?" "Do I feel more energized?" "Is my brain foggy or is it more awake than it was before my meal?" If you feel better than you did before the meal, then the food is good for you. If you feel worse, then you ate something that's bad for you. Or you ate too much. Switch things up until you find what's best.

Exercise is another priceless investment. Something about exerting yourself physically makes you think clearer. My best ideas appear after I've worked up a sweat. The ancients realized this too. Seneca said, "The body should be treated rigorously, that it may not be disobedient to the mind."

When we're stressed or sad, our immediate instinct is to reach for comfort food (read "junk food") or to distract ourselves with mindless entertainment. They provide momentary relief but soon leave us weaker. Next time you feel stressed or down, instead reach for one of Earth's natural uplifters. These are:

- Sunlight
- Sleep
- Fresh air / deep breathing
- Fasting
- Water
- Exercise/Walking

There are very few things the above can't fix. And the more you do them, the better you feel, so the more you'll enjoy them. Hence you're more likely to repeat them, initiating a powerful therapeutic cycle.

When it comes to illness, I like the approach of Via Negativa. Via Negativa means you're not adding cures, simply subtracting the harm. It's a cleaner approach. Think twice before ingesting prescription drugs. They often just mask the symptoms without addressing the root cause of the sickness. Most sickness comes from an excess of something. If you remove the excess, your body finds balance and heals itself.

Consuming less—or less of the bad stuff—is a powerful health agent. Many cultures promote fasting at certain times of the year. Other cultures ban alcohol altogether. This isn't just about religious sacrifice; it's about giving the body and mind time to cleanse itself. It makes for a healthier society.

In America, there's a strong link between poverty and diabetes. Many underlying factors make this so, but it can all be encapsulated this way: those in power benefit from keeping the poor sick. Sugary foods are addictive and easy to produce. They keep customers coming back for more, so they're great for profits. If you can hook a child onto your sweet cereal, you'll have a customer for the next 60 to 70 years.

You also have the secondary industries that benefit from junk food's effects. The healthcare industry would go out of business if no one got sick. Insurance companies need an excuse to keep people paying their premiums. And large employers get away with paying less to their employees if they offer a "good benefits package." The security of employer-subsidized health insurance keeps many would-be entrepreneurs from pursuing their dreams. There isn't an evil plot behind the examples above; it's just how the system has worked itself out throughout the years.

Preventive measures against illness make you better equipped to gain freedom and power. Your mind is clearer. Your body is more energized and light. And your good health attracts attention. Is it any wonder that politicians and CEOs highly groom their image? The hair, the makeup, the teeth whitening, the expensive suits. These are all indirect ways to appear healthier, because we gravitate and support those we believe to be the fittest for survival.

Invest in your health, and your influence naturally increases. When you're full of vigor, your initiatives receive more support, your invitations receive more acceptance, and your words receive more attention. Good health obviously gives you more control internally, but it also gives you more leverage over the outside world. Health is your natural fuel for the journey out of the Fog.

Live Outside but Stay Connected

As we've said earlier, we should avoid mob mentality and the ways of the crowd. But we are a collaborative species, so we must be social. Being a hermit doesn't call to me, and I doubt it calls to you, either. It's a paradox: to become independent, we must interact. As Wallace Wattles wrote: "Getting rich involves the necessity of dealing with men, and of being where there are people to deal with."

I like how Rudyard Kipling puts it in his poem "If": "If you can talk with crowds and keep your virtue."

The secret is coded in there. Talk with crowds, yet keep your virtue. Your innermost philosophy—your virtue—should be shared only with those who are ready to hear it and welcome it. Otherwise, keep it light. Jesus said, "Do not give dogs what is holy, and do not throw your pearls before pigs, lest they trample them underfoot and turn to attack you." Assume others aren't ready until they show you otherwise.

You will only get what you want in direct proportion to how much you help others get what they want. You can only know what others want— and help them get it—through lots of interaction.

Plus, keeping yourself social is the most reliable form of safety. Robert Greene emphasized this with his 18th law of power:

"Isolation exposes you to more dangers
than it Protects you from—
it cuts you off from valuable information,
it makes you conspicuous and
an easy target.
Better to circulate among people,
find allies, mingle.
You are shielded from your
enemies by the crowd."
- Robert Greene in The 48 Laws of Power

To survive in this deceitful world, you must keep your social skills sharp. You must learn to read people. You must learn to spot the lies that could hurt you. You must create allies that benefit from you as much as you benefit from them. You only do this through constant communication.

Don't believe the myth of introverts versus extroverts. Everyone is a little of both. It varies by situation. Certain groups and environments make you feel shyer than others. Extroversion has its benefits and can be grown like a muscle. If not used, it atrophies like a muscle too.

Introversion can also be a superpower. Anyone who follows an intellectual pursuit must develop some introversion muscles. If you can't spend time alone, you will never master any craft. One of my favorite musicians is the late great J Dilla. In my office, I have a framed poster of him working; it inspires me. He was shy and built his chops through countless hours in his basement, practicing alone. His introversion muscles helped him birth a whole genre of music called Lo-Fi. Had he been more social, he would've never endured the thousands of hours of solitary work needed to master his instrument, the Akai MPC.

The world relies on tension and opposites. To me, this is beautiful. A negative often turns into a positive, and vice versa. Because every action has an equal and opposite reaction. Be social, but keep your virtue.

Nietzche's Morality Modes

The Masses prize connection the most, while the Few value independence above all. Each group's strengths and weaknesses derive from their preferences.

The philosopher Friedrich Nietzche explored a similar concept called "Master-slave morality." He argues that there are two fundamental types of morality: "master morality" and "slave morality ." Master morality values pride and power, while slave morality values kindness, empathy, and sympathy. The labels he used are triggering, but the concept is worth examining.

Through nature and nurture, an individual will lean more toward one "morality" over the other. But everyone possesses some of both. Embracing this tension is how we become well-rounded humans.

Leaving the crowd requires that we give up many of the routines and habits we're used to. This will be scary. And justly so. But staying in the Fog would mean ignoring the enormous potential inside of you. Staying in the crowd leads to settling for less than your best.

Although we won't admit it, many of us believe it's better to be poor together than rich alone. Hence, the fear of loneliness keeps us living in Struggleville. But this is a baseless fear. Outside the Fog there are also many chances for deep connection. Anywhere you go there will be a tribe for you. And even if you transcend to a higher level of living, you can always go back and enjoy some time with the Masses.

Robert Greene expressed this sentiment with Power *Law #38: Think as you Like but Behave Like Others*. It's ok to indulge in some fog sparingly if you protect your mental and financial independence accordingly. Venturing back into the Fog should be just an occasional adventure. It's part of the fun of life.

> *"We must be free not because*
> *we claim freedom,*
> *but because we practice it."*
> **- William Faulkner**

Although it's tough to read—and tougher to write—escaping the Fog is an individual sport. You'll encounter others running their own race along the same course, and you can have supporters on the sidelines cheering you on. They can provide nourishment for your journey, but they can't carry you across the finish line. Similarly, you can't carry anyone else; they must do it on their own two legs.

"It's your road, and yours alone.
Others may walk it with you.
But no one can walk it for you."
- Rumi

You will find that many of your close ones won't want to make their own journey. Many are comfortable with their current situation, and that's ok. Maybe they've created a life they can live with. Or perhaps their risk tolerance is low and the adventure scares them.

Fear wears most people down, so they convince themselves they don't want more out of life. You can't force these people to come with you. But also, don't let them keep you in the Fog. They made their choice; you must make your own.

Being Outside the Fog Isn't Easy, but Life Isn't Easy for Anyone

Leaving the Fog is damn hard, yet unbelievably rewarding. Since most quit, escaping puts you in an elite group. The journey makes you more powerful than you can ever imagine.

This new lifestyle will push away a bunch of your closest folks. They won't understand why you reject many of the so-called "pleasures of life." Your family and friends had come to love the person you had always been. They enjoyed the company of your in-the-Fog self, so they have a vested interest in bringing back the "old you."

During get-togethers, they'll ask you why you aren't binge drinking like they are. They'll chuckle when you turn down the triple-fudge chocolate cake. They'll look at you weird when you admit that you haven't been playing the lotto or going to the casino. They'll wonder why you stopped joining them at the nightclub every weekend. Everything I just mentioned will make you feel like a weirdo and a loner, which is why many begin the journey—but few make it out.

This behavior isn't limited to just the human realm. Wild animals do the same. We've all heard about the crabs in a barrel: if you have a bunch of crabs in a bucket, you don't need to put a lid on it before carrying it. If one ever tries to climb out and escape, the others will pull it down. It is unclear whether they do it out of fear for their comrade's life or to grab onto something that will hopefully pull them up. But the lesson is there: trying to leave the crowd isn't always pleasant.

"Ridicule is the tribute paid to the genius by the mediocrities."
- Oscar Wilde

Yet time is the best elixir. These same people who question you will begin to understand your decisions when they wreck their cars and you loan them your second vehicle until theirs gets fixed. They'll thank you when you can offer a job within your company to their graduating son. And they'll realize how much they love you when they get tragic news, and you're the only one by their side consoling them at 2 pm on a Tuesday.

Yes, this way of life is tough. But life is tough for everyone. There's no Easy mode to this game. Mark Manson wrote, "Life is essentially an endless series of problems. The solution to one problem is merely the creation of the next one... Problems never stop, they merely get exchanged and/or upgraded. Happiness comes from solving problems."

So find the problems you enjoy solving, and stick with those.

The answer always comes back to action. Because sometimes, the most severe problem is confusion. Indecision can torment even the strongest mind.

Many authors have written about the paradox of choice. On the surface, we believe more options make us happier, but the opposite is true. A restaurant with too many dishes on the menu can feel like torture. As the modern world increases the number of choices and decisions we have to make, it also increases the stress we experience. Too much choice cripples us because the options foregone linger in our minds. When our chosen path presents any hardship, we convince ourselves we made the wrong choice. This is hell for anyone.

I'm here to free you of this pain.

No choice will ever be perfect. Every decision you make will come with some positives and some negatives.

The key is to have every ounce of your being moving in the same direction. Towards the same goal. A scattered mind is how you lose your marbles.

When you realize there's no "perfect choice," you can focus on what you *can* control: how much energy you put into your follow-through. The abundant flow of your life energy is the source of true happiness.

"You're going to pay a price for
every bloody thing you do
and everything you don't do.
You don't get to choose to not pay a price.
You get to choose which poison
you're going to take. That's it."
- Jordan B. Peterson

With your whole heart, body, and soul finally focused on your journey out of the Fog, the fun can now start. Your senses become sharp. You now spot manipulation you would previously fall for. Your skills of letting go and creating value increase substantially. And this progress excites you. Improving is fun. It is the ultimate thrill in life to find a cause you can give your all to.

Viktor Frankl said it best in Man's Search for Meaning:

*"What man needs is not a tensionless state,
but rather the striving and struggling
for a goal worthy of him."*

Anyone who's discovered lasting happiness will tell you that success fuels passion more than passion fuels success. Ridding yourself of fog puts you on a fast track to success because you've eliminated distractions. You're no longer spinning your wheels on things you have no control over, and you can now concentrate on the places and things you can impact.

But you have to be crystal clear on what you want. You want to have more time, more money, and more control over your life. There is nothing wrong with wanting all of those. They increase life; they attract love, health, and inner peace.

Desire is life seeking fuller expression. A human life's driving force is to channel this expression.

Desire is a great thing—it's the push we all need. Anytime you're not pushing your limits, you won't be happy. But you have to be conscious of why you desire something. Don't chase it just because it's what the crowd is doing. The public values things just because the rest of the crowd values them, not because they're beneficial. Remember when your mom would say, "If everyone is jumping off a bridge, would you also jump off?" Moms know a thing or two.

Desire, when pursued with clarity, leads to progress—because it's in rhythm with life itself. The Universal law of life is growth. Growth of the system. Attach yourself to that foundational principle and you will grow too.

The Enlightened Philosopher Is Always Crucified

I haven't finished telling you about Plato's Allegory of the Cave.

As mentioned earlier, Plato believed most humans live at the bottom of a metaphorical cave. And all we've ever known are the shadows of fake figurines we see projected onto the wall by the people who run our government and major institutions. The Few who dare to escape from the bottom of this cave are faced with a choice: they can stop at the next level up, where they see the Puppeteers creating the shadows, or they can continue climbing up the cave until they reach the Outside.

Once the Few philosophers reach the Outside, they finally see the sun and are temporarily blinded by all this light. Since they've lived inside a cave all these years, they are not used to the sun's brightness.

But slowly, their eyes adjust to the sun's light. Now they see real animals and trees and the true nature of reality. They see something few ever witness. They see how great reality is.

Here is where we left off in our story.

Now, the freed prisoner's first impulse is to go back and alert the Masses inside the cave about how wonderful the Outside world is. In the same way you love putting your friends onto new songs, or taking your colleagues to a hip new restaurant, we relish sharing cool things. But Plato warns us about what happens next.

If the freed philosopher returns to the cave to tell others, he can't see anything. He is temporarily blind because his eyes are now used to the sun's brightness. Upon arrival, the prisoners inside the cave notice his condition and suspect that his journey outside the cave harmed him. While he's trying to tell them about the Outside, they think he's delirious. This makes them believe that they're better off staying put. The worst aspect of human nature then takes over. The prisoners label the philosopher a sick and crazy madman, and they eventually kill him.

The life of a true philosopher is a dangerous one. When you join the Few, expect hate.

> *"Lord, protect me from my friends;*
> *I can take care of my enemies."*
> **- Voltaire**

Send Paper Planes

As one of the Few, we will be tempted to go back into the cave and rescue our tribe. I advise you that this is the wrong approach.

The Masses aren't ready for someone who challenges their beliefs. Being too direct is a recipe for ruin. Many honorable folks have paid for this with their life. It's what happened to Socrates. And to Jesus. And to Malcolm X.

Increasingly during your escape—and even more pronounced once Outside—you'll gain the disapproval of most around you. They don't want you to change. Although they won't admit it, they fear you'll change too much and forget about them.

They don't yet understand that your escape puts you in a better position to help *them* out down the line. So they will first use all their powers of persuasion to get you to stay put. If the "nice" way doesn't work, they will move on to shady tactics. They will put you down and call you names. They will stop supporting you. People do ugly things out of fear.

Beyond your immediate circle, your tribe and community will fight you tooth and nail. In a way, they too, are afraid. They are scared because your actions are challenging their limited view of the world. They aren't ready to see reality yet.

This is why we've stated that life Outside the Fog will sometimes be lonely. And re-entering the Fog is dangerous to the point of being fatal. Only a select Few will understand your actions, and often you have no way of parsing who's who.

Once out of the Fog, our only choice is to report back through third parties in subtle ways. I call it "sending paper planes." You scribble wise words on paper and fold it up for flight. Then launch it off.

To reach the Masses, use the same avenues as the Puppeteers. Yes, your message will be mostly drowned out. You'll never be able to compete on quantity, so don't even try. Your advice gets lost like a needle in a haystack, but if it's quality, someone will eventually find that needle. And they'll appreciate it for what it is.

That's the best-case scenario you can hope for.

I've found one of those needles in the haystack. Maybe it's still too direct, but this is my attempt at a paper plane.

"Tell all the truth but tell it slant —
Success in Circuit lies
Too bright for our infirm Delight
The Truth's superb surprise
As Lightning to the Children eased
With explanation kind
The Truth must dazzle gradually
Or every man be blind"
- Emily Dickinson

CHAPTER 7:
POWER AND INFLUENCE:
HOW TO GET WHAT YOU WANT

Robert Greene said the first step toward becoming rational is understanding our fundamental irrationality. As individuals, we often act *against our best interests* and let emotions take the wheel. This means we are regularly the originators of our pain and suffering without explanation for why.

Take, for example, how we treat others:

> *"It is a general rule of human nature*
> *that people despise those*
> *who treat them well,*
> *and look up to those*

who make no concessions."

- Thucydides

As Thucydides noticed thousands of years ago, humans act backward. When someone's nice to us, we tend to devalue and repay them with hostility. Meanwhile, those who hurt us seem to receive our best treatment. It happens in friendships, in love, in business, and in our family dynamics as well.

I have my own theory on why humans behave so strangely towards others. And it has multiple layers to it.

Let's peel back this onion.

Firstly, we act irrationally because we don't see the birdseye view of our environment. All we see is what's immediate, what's in front of us right now. A great example is the Parable of the Blind Men and the Elephant. A group of blind men were asked to describe an elephant. One of them touched the animal's side and described it as "Smooth. Like a wall!" Another put out his hand and felt the trunk, so he said an elephant is "round and skinny, like a snake." A third one touched its tusk and said, "An elephant is sharp, like a spear." Each thought the other two were purposely lying, so they argued and eventually came to blows.

We are like those blind men. We rarely consider that our perspective might be limited. Instead, we quickly jump to conclusions about the intentions of others. In doing so, we often hurt those who want to help and adore those who hurt us.

We've all heard the saying, "Don't kill the messenger." Someone with good intentions will try to alert us of oncoming danger, but we don't like bad news, so we'll foolishly hurt them. Meanwhile, many undercover enemies will jump at the chance to deliver any good news, knowing we'll associate them with this welcome information. Our problem is that we have no concrete way to zoom out of our life and see the bigger game playing out around us. Unless we control our shortsightedness, we will continue acting backward. And continue proving correct the axiom "no good deed goes unpunished."

Secondly, our fears color our perspective. Past troubles have left us scarred and traumatized. We'll do anything to avoid going through those things again, so we load up our defense mechanisms over the scars. We bark at anyone who even reminds us of past pain. It becomes paranoia. We start misreading signals. In time, everything others say and do takes on the hue of our trauma. It's the classic example of the returning soldier who has Post-Traumatic Stress Disorder. Everything others say and do gets filtered through the fear. A scared dog will often bite the hand that feeds it.

The third and final reason humans act backward goes back to how this book opened: the world is full of deception. We remember how we've deceived others before, and it turns us into cynics. How can we trust others to be truthful if *we've* lied and gotten away with it? It's much safer, we tell ourselves, to assume everyone else is lying. So when someone does something nice for us, we suspect their intentions aren't so genuine. We believe they're trying to soften us and get what they're after. In trying to protect ourselves, we now hurt this person.

Meanwhile, people who mistreat us receive our kindest treatment. We rationalize that they're not looking for anything from us. We also assume they are of higher status since they don't care to please us. Which implies they're in a position to help *us* with their abundance. At this point, our auto-pilot kicks in. We put on our deceptive mask and treat this perceived "higher-level" person nicely. If we gain enough favor—we believe—they might share their wealth with us. So they get our best smiles and favors and friendly gestures.

It's a vicious, never-ending cycle. You treat me nicely. I don't trust your niceness. So I mistreat you. My bad behavior makes you think I don't want anything from you. Believing I want nothing from you, you assume I must have more resources than you. And now you will treat me nicely, hoping to gain future favors. The cycle continues. On and on and on.

Remember this: humans only admire strength, and we despise the weak. Those "above us" get our best, while those "below" get our worst. Following this logic, we see why Robert Greene wrote, "Trying to please people less will make them more likely in the long run to respect and treat you better."

Emphasis on *the long run*.

In the short run, those you neglect might kick, scream, and act annoyed. But this is just an act. Don't fall for it. They are simply lashing out as a last-ditch effort to fool you. This behavior soon settles, and the new status quo gets established.

The Sport of All Sports: The Status Game

The one game all humans play—whether we admit it to ourselves or not—is the status game. Minute by minute, we're evaluating who's up, who's down, and who can help us gain more status. This concept lives in our minds rent-free. So our every behavior tilts towards things we think will get us access to high-status individuals. We want to gain their favor, so we try to please them.

However, if we're talking cold, hard strategy—there's a more direct route. If you want to gain favor, then the target must believe you hold higher status than they do overall. Or at least in a realm they value. This way, they have something to gain from the interaction. With enough incentive, they will bend to your will. It's basic self-interest.

This is the essence of interpersonal dynamics: the pursuit of higher status.

Scientists will tell you that humans, at their core, aim for survival. Food, shelter, sex—all these basic needs seem to lead back to survival. But even more fundamental than those needs is status. The more status we have within our tribe, the more security we enjoy. It gives us more access to good food, fancier houses, and better mating opportunities. For better or worse, everything we do ultimately boils down to a desire for higher status.

In this world of countless competitions, one contest rules above all. We are all ultimately playing the status game.

Once we can own up to the fact that we're playing the status game, we can then strategize on gaining an edge. Or for the genuine among us, we can at least defend ourselves against those who want to derail us. Maybe you don't want to be a conqueror, but you also don't want to be conquered. So you must play.

The foundation of a status strategy is simple: make others believe your status is higher than it really is, or at least higher than *theirs*.

This takes some subtle deception. And the deception is this: the less you seem to care what people think, the better stuff they think. When they see you're nonchalant, they become convinced you have nothing to gain from associating with them. It elevates you in their scoreboard. In romantic seduction, this takes the form of playing hard to get or subtle reverse psychology. In school, it's the popular troublemaker. A lack of regard appears to signal an abundance of resources. And voila! Higher status.

Realize also: status is a two-sided affair. To sustain the game, your own mind must sense the trick is working, even if it requires a bit of self-delusion.

> *"I am not what I think I am,*
> *and I am not what you think I am.*
> *I am what I think you think I am."*
> **- Charles Horton Cooley**

The Rep Rope

A word of caution. Remember that chasing status is ultimately a game. And all games involve some losses. Your reputation is your "record," so occasionally, it'll take a hit. No one who's lived fully has ever gotten out with a flawless reputation. And neither will you.

Don't let fear stop you from taking risks. Don't get roped into captivity by your own rep.

Lack of boldness is a surefire way to lose the respect of others and yourself. No one respects the meek. We might "like" them because they're predictable and pose no threat to us, but the timid never build up the social capital needed to achieve big goals.

What good is having people like you if they won't help you? Respect takes you farther.

Reputations are much more resilient than we think. People are more forgiving than you'd expect. And time has a way of changing villains into heroes and heroes into villains. Remember, reality is gray, and we all fall somewhere within that spectrum. No one is a pure white knight or a jet-black heel.

The spotless reputations we were born with— just like our bodies—are meant to be blemished and worn away. Picture wearing an all-white outfit to an outdoor event. If your clothes are still spotless at the end of the day, you didn't dance, play, or have as much fun as you should've. You might be ok with that, but it's not my idea of a good time.

I don't aim to be a saint to everyone, just a helper to those I care for. They'll know I'm coming from a good place. As for everyone else, I'm sure they'll look for reasons to drag my name in the mud.

As Gerald Peters often says: "I'm only looking for the people who are looking for me." Which he follows with: "You don't like what I said? Ok, bye!"

Heavy is the head that wears the crown. Not all your decisions will be winners. Sometimes it's about picking the lesser of two evils.

All status brings with it both fans and haters. Great people take up more space, so they attract more attention, good and bad. Attention is the oxygen to your movement. As 50 Cent raps, "I need you. I need you to hate, so I can use you for your energy."

Haters are the ying to your supporters' yang.

In reality, haters are just confused souls. They hate on you because your actions resemble their brand of deception, and it makes them self-conscious. Psychologists point out that the qualities we hate most in others are qualities we are fighting to conceal in ourselves. Haters are scared you could topple their house of cards. Or they're jealous you're getting away with it when they can't. Thus, they hate.

As children, my younger brother was more crafty than I was. And way bolder. Kids are always attracted to what's off-limits. If I ever took something from Dad's dresser, my little brother would threaten me: "Ooh, wait until I tell Mom and Dad. They'll spank you." This would scare me, so I'd put the thing down. Within seconds he'd pick it up, taunting me as he played with fire. I would threaten to tell just like he did, but he didn't care. He was the baby. He had immunity. And on the few occasions he got punished, his ego wouldn't bruise like mine. I feared disappointing my parents. He didn't. So he enjoyed the freedom I envied. Towards my brother, I was a hater.

Hate is just a demand for better deception. Masterful deception is the only kind we respect, the only thing we'll yield to.

"When you show yourself to the world
and display your talents,
you naturally stir all kinds of
resentment, envy, and other
manifestations of insecurity...
you cannot spend your life worrying
about the petty feelings of others."
- Robert Greene, The 48 Laws of Power

Life demands we become internally resilient. All power starts first from the inside:

"Whatever people do, feel, think, or say,
don't take it personally.

If they tell you how wonderful you are,
they are not saying that because of you.
You know you are wonderful.
It is not necessary to believe other people
who tell you that you are wonderful."
- Don Miguel Ruiz, The Four Agreements

Everyone lives in their own inner world, which is never the same as anyone else's. You'll never really know what others are thinking, so you might as well do as you please. Only bold moves will make them show their hand.

Remember: the less you seem to care what people think, the better stuff they think. A need for validation reveals that you're in the Fog, so it lowers your status. Others assume you have little to offer. They move on. But when you don't seek external validation, it attracts admiration.

I've always loved the saying, "The easily shamed will never learn." I add, "If you never try, you'll never know."

So stop worrying so much about what others think. You're here for a purpose. You're here to provide value to your community in a way only you can. If you do this, others will make room for your personality. The key is to focus on delivering value. And you don't measure value by reputation; you measure it with the money and time others give you in return. Because people only spend money and time on the things that are important to them. The other stuff is just hot air.

The Two-Way Person: Are These Principles Evil?

Is playing the status game evil?

Are all humans evil because we sometimes use deception to get our way?

Are we just left with two choices, to be either "crafty and evil" or "naive and saintly"?

The answer to all of the above is a resounding "NO."

Playing the status game isn't being evil; it's being human.

Each of us is as deceitful as we feel we must be to survive. Survival means avoiding fog. The more you avoid fog, the less pressure you'll be under, and the freer you'll be to act as a force for growth in this world.

Humans aren't evil for using deception. Humans are evil if their deception is purely for their individual benefit. When you tell white lies to spare others' feelings—and when you play the hands that life deals—you're interacting with reality in its preferred language. You are simply a realist. Realism is the highest form of living and can serve generous or selfish ends. You're on the right track if you're operating from a place of generosity.

It's time to replace the long-held notion of the "bad apple" with a better explanation: the "bad barrel." The real blame falls on our social setting and the system, not the individual. We got put in a bad barrel, and that bad barrel is life in the Fog.

You can sit and cry about it. Or you can work with what you have, develop your Rich Instinct, and work on your escape. Escaping gives you more leverage to turn around and help others.

If you're too weak and empty from being exploited, you have no resources to help others.

Your aim is to become strong. Remember, deep down, people are only attracted to strength, while they're put off by weakness. They will say they admire gentleness and humility, but they really only admire it coming from those who also already have power.

"It has always seemed strange to me...
the things we admire in men,
kindness and generosity, openness,
honesty, understanding and feeling,
are the concomitants of failure
in our system.
And those traits we detest,
sharpness, greed, acquisitiveness,
meanness, egotism and self-interest,
are the traits of success.
And while men admire the quality
of the first they
love the produce of the second."
- John Steinbeck

To build and maintain your strength, learn to manage your resources. As mentioned before, Karma is real, so what you put out comes back to you multiplied. When you give, you will receive multiplied.

However, you must give mainly to the deserving, and do so without completely drying up your reserves. It's ok to be considered stingy. Machiavelli said that one who is too generous isn't appreciated and only causes his beneficiaries to grow greedy for more. At this pace, resources will soon be exhausted. If you then start to limit your giving, you'll soon be called "stingy" in a louder way than had you never given to begin with. Humans get angrier about losing something they once had than they are motivated to gain something that's never been theirs.

If you give too much to the point you exhaust your reserves, you may need to borrow from some of those same people you previously gave generously to. And they will resent you much more for this reversal.

Best to give just enough so that your surplus isn't depleted. You are the best steward of your fortune. As you maintain it, you'll also learn how to multiply it. Once multiplied, then you can give more in the future.

The Art of Getting What You Want

The longer you live, the more you accept the old axiom: It's not what you do that matters; it's how you do it. Living is not a science; it's an art form. And like all art, it can be graceful or clumsy.

To live gracefully, you must do everything with power and boldness behind it. Actions imbued with these qualities will succeed much more often than they fail. And on the few occasions they fail, the momentum you carry will allow you to switch gears easily into a plan B.

Boldness has a flair and style to it. And style makes life worth living. I love these lines from Charles Bukowski:

"Style is the answer to everything,
A fresh way to approach a dull
or dangerous thing,
To do a dull thing with style is preferable
to doing a dangerous thing without it,
To do a dangerous thing with style
is what I call art."

Life itself is risky and dangerous. No one gets out alive. To live with style is an art.

Part of the *how* also applies to what you say. In your journey out of the Fog, you'll have to deliver bad news from time to time. You'll also have to verbally push some people out of your way to prevent violence. In both these cases, remember: you can get away with saying anything as long as your delivery is impeccable.

Some situations call for a lighter touch or an indirect route. Some require an iron fist inside a silk glove. Some require a rugged bluff. Everyone has a way in; it's just about finding it. There is no foolproof way to know in advance what these magic words are; it simply requires experience dealing with all sorts of people. As mentioned earlier: keep social. Keep interacting.

Saying yes to something means you're saying no to other things. For this reason, you'll have to say "no" to many unimportant things so you can say yes and focus on the important ones. Learn the right ways to say no.

On this, Baltasar Gracian has some advice for us:

"Some men's No is thought more of
than the Yes of others:
for a gilded No is more satisfactory
than a dry Yes.
There are some who always
have No on their lips,
whereby they make everything distasteful.

No always comes first with them,
and when sometimes they
give way after all,
it does them no good on account
of the unpleasing herald.
Your refusal need not be point-blank:
let the disappointment come by degrees.
Nor let the refusal be final;
that would be to destroy dependence;
let some spice of hope remain
to soften the rejection.
Let politeness compensate and
fine words supply the place of deeds."

Once you've gotten good at saying no indirectly, you'll also learn that there are some occasions where simply saying less is the best approach:

"When you are trying to
impress people with words,
the more you say,
the more common you appear,
and the less in control.
Even if you are saying something banal,
it will seem original if you make it vague,

135

open-ended, and sphinxlike.
Powerful people impress and
intimidate by saying less.
The more you say,
the more likely you are
to say something foolish."
- Robert Greene, The 48 Laws of Power

More important than words, though, are actions. Actions are the bedrock on which you can build pretty word castles. Someone who never backs up their promises will soon lose the attention and trust of everyone. Your verbal maneuvers will only work if your target trusts that the words will manifest into real-life events.

Assuming they trust your word, the key to getting what you want from others is to also help them get what *they* want. Self-interest is the motivator to rely on. If you are perceived to have something of value— or are known to be helpful—you will never have a shortage of friends. You will never lack helping hands when you need them.

You'll automatically amass value by aiming to rid your life of fog since the Fog steals your money, time, health, peace of mind, and focus. When you stop giving these away carelessly, you instantly have more value to offer others. This value attracts supporters who want to tap into what you have.

This is why being perceived as a high-status individual is so powerful.

As we mentioned earlier, status is the one thing *everyone* wants more of. And how you carry yourself is a big signaling factor of status. Someone calm and deliberate with their words automatically projects higher status than they would without these qualities. Someone who isn't trying too hard to please others gives the impression that their value is more tangible than just being "nice." It signals deeper importance. And this sense of mystery works to your advantage. Don't reveal all your gifts, so others never know your limits. Let their imagination roam: the bulk of your value is hidden under the surface. You want to be an iceberg.

When you relax and stop being desperate, the whole world opens up to you.

"As soon as you stop wanting something,
you get it."
- Andy Warhol

Now you understand why so many people can fake their way to the top, right? They model the persona of someone powerful, and through favors, slowly trade up the social food chain. Once outside the Fog, you will have so much real value that your demeanor doesn't need any more faking. As they say, "real recognize real."

The way to get rich and powerful in this world is to be both strong and smart. To be both a Lion and a Fox.

"The lion cannot guard himself
from the toils, nor the fox from wolves.
A Prince must therefore be a fox
to discern toils,
and a lion to drive off wolves."
- Niccolo Machiavelli in The Prince

The way to get both strong and smart is to avoid fog as much as possible since fog debilitates our body and mind. Outside the Fog, you are closest to reality, so your actions are congruent with nature, whereas the Masses are tripped up by their fantasies.

"The way men live is so far removed
from the way they ought to live that

anyone who abandons what is
for what should be
pursues his downfall rather
than his preservation;
for a man who strives after goodness
in all his acts is sure to come to ruin,
since there are so many
men who are not good."

- *Niccolo Machiavelli* in *The Prince*

Doing what reality calls for is the most effective action we can take.

And the measure of effectiveness all depends on our time horizon.

Long-term results are usually the complete opposite of an action's short-term effects. An uncomfortable conversation with a friend today might leave a bitter taste in everyone's mouth for the moment, but down the line, that friend will respect you more for helping them grow. Short-term pain must not be avoided if you aim to build long, fruitful relationships.

This general rule of thumb was coined by the marketing genius Al Ries. He called it The Law of Perspective, which illustrated how marketing moves that increase revenue for a company in the short term usually hurt business in the long term. For example, sales discounts increase customer purchases immediately, but in the long run, it hurts the brand because you're educating customers not to buy at regular prices. It subconsciously communicates that your normal prices are too high; otherwise, the items would've sold out before the sale even happened.

If you're smart, you'll focus on winning over the long term. It might mean forfeiting the battle so you can win the war. Gary Vee calls it "Jab-Jab-Jab-Right Hook." You lead by giving—by creating goodwill—and it all bears fruit down the line.

*"This is the secret sauce to
getting what you want.
All the benefits in life come
from compound interest.
Whether it's in relationships,
or making money, or in learning...
One should pick an industry where
you can play long-term games
with long-term people."*
- Naval Ravikant

Jerry Saltz calculated that a prosperous career in the arts often relies on just 12 strategic supporters. In many cases, even less. On a basic level, this applies to all areas of life. The key is to have this group of supporters *really* like you and be in it for the long haul. They will promote your work and open doors for you. And these doors lead to all your big scores.

It's clear to see, successful networks are more about intensity than extensity. A few strong relationships instead of many weak ones. But strong relationships require time to bear fruit.

We should be thinking long-term in our personal life too. If we give away our affection and energy and time to the first person who shows us any little interest, we're communicating that our love is cheap. Sure, we'll get some attention in the short term; but that appreciation soon fades when they find someone who places a higher value on themselves.

In simplest terms, getting what we want is about dealing with other humans as reality has made them, not as we'd like them to be. When we're able to get their attention through boldness, communicate with them using just the right words (and not more), learn how to say "no" gracefully, and hold their interest long-term by placing a high value on what we offer, then the world will be ours.

CHAPTER 8:
YOU ARE WHAT YOU RISK:
HOW COURAGE DEFINES
US

O nce upon a time, the world was much more lopsided. Information, knowledge, and technology were previously only available to the upper crust of society. Today, everyone has access to the above in first-world countries (and many others).

Google now holds more information than all human brains combined. And your phone can process algorithms that were impossible just two generations ago. Everyone with a working smartphone can access the world's knowledge and computing power. In developed nations, only a few select advantages separate the elite from the Masses.

Sure, the money and connections of the rich will always hold power. Still, the strongest force any human can ever tap into is courage.

The Universe has always had an abundance of everything, except courage. That's why it's so valuable, because it's scarce. Courage is the great equalizer. With enough courage, you can get the money and connections needed to reach your goals.

> *"Courage is the human virtue*
> *that counts most —*
> *courage to act on limited knowledge*
> *and insufficient evidence.*
> *That's all any of us have."*
> **- Robert Frost**

Characters like Harry Potter, Katniss Everdeen, and Spider-Man, are all based on the same belief. Their creators understood that all heroes must possess courage. Lajos Egri outlined it this way. "A man whose fear is greater than his desire, or a man who has no great, all-consuming passion, or one who has patience and does not oppose, cannot be a pivotal character." The hero can be lacking in any other area. In fact, they *must* be imperfect to be likable. They don't always have to be smart, kind, physically strong, or charismatic. But they *must always* transcend their fear.

And so must we. If we want to be the main character of our life.

As mentioned earlier, your path to money and power and health and inner peace—your way out of the Fog—is unlocked with courage. It takes courage to say "no" to the vices of society. It takes courage to withstand peer pressure from friends and family. It also takes major courage to ignore the world's mirages and follow your gut. It's safe to move with the Masses but totally scary to give up safety and join the Few.

"You think it'd be better if things were easy.
You wish you didn't have to take this risk.
If only the leap didn't
look so damn dangerous.
That's just the fear talking.
It's good that it's hard.
It deters the cowards
and it intrigues the courageous."
- **Ryan Holiday in Courage is Calling**

We all know what courage is. And we've all displayed it from time to time. Yet the word "courage" itself sounds abstract. It's not. At its core, courage is simply a special mix of sacrifice and risk. To exhibit courage, you merely have to make a sacrifice in one area of your life so that you can be risky in another. Essentially, courage is just a reallocation of your energy. Take some energy from here, and put it there.

For me, this new definition blew the locks off the door.

To leave the Fog and reach your goals, there is no way around courage. Cutting out your TV watching, cutting out toxic friends, and cutting out junk food; it all takes courage. Those things are so embedded into modern life that you'll be ridiculed for passing on them. The simple question is: are you brave enough to live with the ridicule? Or will you cower back into life as the Masses live it?

Ignore those who say life should be one way or another, those who put rails on life. Life is whatever *you* want to make of it. It's not what your friends or family want. Your highest purpose is to help others, but to do it in *your* unique way. In a way that only you can. Thomas Edison helped in his unique way.

So did Richard Pryor. The same goes for Mother Theresa. None of them were perfect, but they were brave enough to follow their own path.

When all is said and done, you will be defined by how you exhibited courage. You are what you risk.

Bring something that hasn't been brought to the table before. You do this through your own blend of courage. I don't know what that looks like for you. All I know is you won't find it inside the Fog. *You'll* have to color outside the lines for some time—maybe a month, a year, or a decade—to complete that mission. The time frame is different for everyone. But there will be a moment to ditch the rails. Otherwise, you won't find your contribution to the growth of the Universe.

Joseph Campbell laid out the blueprint for the Hero's Journey. The hero always starts in their known world—their village—and after a bout with fear, they finally venture into the unknown to look for the solution to the village's problem. Through much sacrifice and struggle, they finally find the magic elixir and bring it back to the known world. The hero is welcomed back by their village as a savior. They are a leader now. The journey has transformed them. Physically they're back home like before, but mentally they're out of the Fog.

Think back to chapter three and Plato's cave. He taught that all we see is an illusion of the world projected for us by the Puppeteers who keep society indoctrinated. To escape this lower level of the cave, we must block out these images and navigate by "feeling." Well, as we mentioned earlier, you gain a feel for things only through hands-on experimentation. Through trial and error, and learning to follow your gut.

If you are scared of trial and error—or are easily shamed—remember that no one is born fearless. Fearlessness must be developed like a muscle.

I love how Mellody Hobson put it. She said, "Bravery is not the absence of fear; it is overcoming it." Without experiencing fear, you can't display bravery. Being brave, by default, requires that you *feel fear*. And that you proceed anyway.

> *"Far better it is to dare mighty things,*
> *to win glorious triumphs,*
> *even though checkered by failure,*
> *than to take rank with those poor spirits who*
> *neither enjoy much nor suffer much,*

because they live in the gray twilight
that knows not victory nor defeat."
- Theodore Roosevelt

Nietzsche hinted at the same when he said, "Become who you are." He understood that most individuals live out-of-sync with their essence just to fit in with their tribe's expectations. They live this way due to fear. Only by pushing against that fear do you become who you are. Who you are afraid to become.

"Risk is an essential need of the soul.
The absence of risk produces
a kind of boredom
which paralyzes in a different way
from fear, but almost as much."
- Simone Weil

More often than I care to admit, I get paralyzed by fear. But the moment I take any small step forward, I snap out of it. I then start doing more, and the fear leaves. I start caring less about single-event outcomes because each is now a smaller part of my life as a whole. That's the formula. The more you do, the less you care.

> *"Action is a great restorer*
> *and builder of confidence.*
> *Inaction is not only the result,*
> *but the cause, of fear.*
> *Perhaps the action you take*
> *will be successful;*
> *perhaps different action or*
> *adjustments will have to follow.*
> *But any action is better*
> *than no action at all."*
> **- Norman Vincent Peale**

Think about how insurance companies operate. They collect small amounts of money from tons and tons of small customers. A few of these customers will have significant accidents which require a payout of millions of dollars from the insurance company. But the vast majority will never have a big accident. In this way, the insurance company brings its risk close to zero by spreading it across large numbers. You should look at your life this way. Be cautious never to wipe out entirely. Don't risk things that could cause irreparable damage to your health, your close relationships, or your standing as a law-abiding citizen. Most other mistakes can be minimized and reversed with some more boldness, time, and cunning.

"Your fears are a kind of prison
that confines you within
a limited range of action.
The less you fear,
the more power you will have
and the more fully you will live."
- Robert Greene in The 50th Law

Tim Urban created a great diagram to display the spectrum of risk. He called it "The Danger Scale." On the scale, things within the 1 - 4 range are those everyone can agree aren't dangerous. In the 7 - 10 range fall the clearly dangerous things that everyone can agree on. But then there's the middle of the scale in the 4 - 7 range, which he calls "The Chef Lab." The general population considers these things dangerous, but they're not actually dangerous. He says our success depends on doing things within the Chef Lab range because those are both safe and rewarding. There isn't much value in living within the 1-4 range since those are the things everyone else is doing.

The Danger Scale

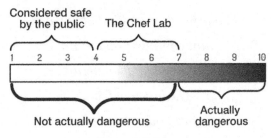

Courtesy of: Tim Urban

Despite what things may seem like right now, most obstacles between you and your goals aren't as unmovable as you think. We perceive them as immovable because we're looking at the shadows around us. But the moment we take bold action, the resistance gives way much easier than we expect. The emphasis is on *bold* action. However, if we take the logical steps that the Masses would take, our obstacles won't budge an inch. This is why your instinct—and feeling things out—will always yield better results than going by what you see. The value is in action that is odd, bold, and scarce.

We run from fear when in reality, fear is a great compass. What we fear doing most is usually what we most need to do. As the Britsh Special Air Service motto goes, "Who dares, wins." Because daring action is the single thing that will move the needle.

> *"I got every ingredient;*
> *all I need is the courage."*
> **- Eminem in the song "8 Mile"**

Al Ries calls it The Law of Singularity. History teaches us that the only thing that works in business (and life) is the single, bold stroke. Furthermore, in any given situation, there is only one move that will produce substantial results. This is the place where the resistance is vulnerable. That place should be the focus of your efforts. As he puts it, what works is simple: the unexpected.

I call it *One Bold Move*. Whenever you're feeling stuck, or a situation looks unfixable, performing One Bold Move is the way through. It will be unorthodox and unexpected—and will cause you to feel fear—but afterward, you'll get the results you're aiming for. Believe that.

What makes One Bold Move magical is that even if it fails, The Universe often steps in to carry you through. Boldness is so scarce that any display of it attracts immediate attention. As your face is down in the mud, help swoops in from all angles. Your actions entertain and encourage the Masses, so they support you.

Meanwhile, the Few are mobilized to help by a different emotion. They feel a kinship. When they see someone taking bold action, they step in to help. They remember what it's like. And what better allies to have on your side than those who own everything?

This is the power of courage. It recruits energy from everywhere and puts it at your fingertips.

"Nature loves courage.
You make the commitment
and nature will respond
to that commitment by
removing impossible obstacles.
Dream the impossible dream and
the world will not grind you under,
it will lift you up.
This is the trick. This is what all these teachers and
philosophers who really counted,

who really touched the alchemical gold,
this is what they understood.
This is the shamanic dance in the waterfall. This is
how magic is done.
By hurling yourself into the abyss
and discovering it's a feather bed."
~ Terence McKenna

There is no reason not to be courageous. There is no reason to stay down after you fall. There is no reason to hold back your One Bold Move. What you're looking for is on the other side of fear. What you're looking for is looking for you.

"Run from what's comfortable.
Forget safety.
Live where you fear to live.
Destroy your reputation.
Be notorious.
I have tried prudent planning
long enough.
From now on I'll be mad."
- Rumi

CHAPTER 9:
THE PHILOSOPHY OF THE RICH AND POWERFUL: INTENSE REALISM

The rich and powerful rule over society because their guiding philosophy is far superior to that of the Masses. The Masses—whether they own up to it or not—live for escapism. Meanwhile, the Few are on a constant search for reality. It's a philosophy I call *Intense Realism.* Its cornerstone is to avoid the Fog at all costs and instead see things for what they are. Robert Greene said it best in *The 50th Law* when he wrote, "The firmer your grasp on reality, the more power you will have to alter it for your purposes."

To be powerful is to have a certain level of control over yourself and others. Anyone who lacks control of themselves will never have control over others. Only by first obtaining dominion over yourself can you begin to influence the world around you.

The powerful can will themselves to do the difficult things most folks won't—so they can have the things most can't. One of these difficult things: overcoming addiction. If you are addicted to something, your judgment is clouded, and eventually you will lose control over yourself. A person addicted to sweets loses the capacity to say no when a treat is offered to them. They can't step into a convenience store without buying candy.

If left unchecked, this addiction soon starts rotting their life. Their health starts to suffer, causing their confidence to suffer, causing them to shy away from challenging activities, and causing them to lose influence within their circle. Then the tide reverses. They start being influenced more and more by the decisions of others. Before they know it, they've lost all power. They are now the low man on the totem pole.

But the powerful rid themselves of addictions. It starts with a small win, followed by more small victories. This gives them a thrill. The best kind. The thrill that comes from doing something difficult. It gives them more positive energy. Soon, all internal challenges have been conquered, and they are now free to work on external challenges. They start gaining control over their environment: things, places, and people around them. When a self-assured person talks, others pay attention.

Addictions that steal your power are fog. The more fog you have around you, the less in touch you are with reality, so your actions become increasingly clumsy. You become like a baby who can't stand up on their legs. While those outside the Fog are like the parents a baby relies on.

Power is, therefore, inversely proportional to the amount of fog in one's life. More fog equals less power. Less fog equals more power.

"Reality is my drug. The more I have of it, the more power I get and the higher I feel."
—50 Cent

More than simply avoiding fog, the rich and powerful first fill their life with *presence*. Being completely and utterly present in the moment is *the* competitive advantage of all advantages.

Presence is being fully immersed in the moment. It means focusing on what you're doing right now while blocking out all distractions the modern world throws at you. When you're fully present, everything you do has more value because it has the full force of your being embedded into it. A scattered mind causes you to make mistakes. And it opens the door to being deceived and lied to.

> *"There is no surer sign in the world*
> *of a little, weak mind,*
> *than inattention.*
> *Whatever is worth doing at all,*
> *is worth doing well;*
> *and nothing can be well done*
> *without attention."*
> **- Lord Chesterfield in letters to his son**

Presence of mind is part and parcel of power. The power of *now* is the only thing you have, don't waste it with distractions.

> *"You don't set out to build a wall.*
> *You don't say 'I'm going to build*
> *the biggest, baddest, greatest wall*

that's ever been built. '
You don't start there.
You say 'I'm gonna lay this brick
as perfectly as a brick can be laid,'
and you do that every single day,
and soon you have a wall."
- Will Smith

It's Not About Good Versus Evil;
It's About Reality Versus Fantasy

The powerful also avoid another trap: the temptation to judge things as good or evil.

Although it would simplify things, the world is sadly not black and white. As we mentioned earlier, reality is shades of gray.

Realize: labels like "good" or "evil" change with time, place, and perspective. In certain parts of the world, it is good and respectable for a man to have multiple wives. In most of America, it'd be considered a crime. A woman's right to abort a child has gone from illegal to legal to illegal throughout the years. Although stealing has always been considered wrong, the laws around what is "mine" versus what's "ours" fluctuates by nation. The examples are countless. What is right and wrong changes with the culture and who's leading the government.

> *"Jesus Christ said: 'Resist not evil,'*
> *for He knew in reality,*
> *there is no evil,*
> *therefore nothing to resist."*
> **- Florence Scovel Shinn**

You must keep an open mind to the changes around you since you'll notice that aging also adjusts your stance. Science has found that the human body replenishes each of its cells every seven years. You have not *one* single cell in common with the *you* from seven years ago. You're a walking mass of change. To succeed, you must be open to change while still holding some core principles.

So if Good vs. Evil isn't a resilient system, then what *should* be our method of judgment? Simple. The one principle that should anchor you is an intense thirst for reality since reality, by definition, flows with the Universe.

Your barometer should measure whether a thing is in accordance with reality or fantasy. Remember that reality is about growth for the system, which takes precedence over growth for an individual. Reality is rough around the edges, full of grit and resistance—things that engender strength. In contrast, fantasy appears smooth and sterile. Fantasy advertises an image of paradise that shuns effort and work, thereby stunting growth.

The "perfect" families you see in TV shows are a fantasy. The show *Friends*, with its aspirational young urbanite lifestyle, is alluring—but it's fantasy. How can Phoebe, Rachel, and Monica afford a spacious West Village apartment on low-paying jobs while still having loads of free time to hang out at a coffee shop? How does Joey chip in with his part of the rent if he is mostly out of work? It makes for entertaining TV but sets you up for a letdown. The material perks of that lifestyle are certainly attainable, but for a much higher price than the characters seem to pay.

If an action is in accordance with reality, it is desirable and wise. Whereas if it makes you fall out of step with the rhythm of nature, you should consider it undesirable and foolish.

The ancient Stoic philosophers lived by a term called Amor Fati. Its literal translation is "love of fate." It's a powerful concept that urges one to embrace everything that happens, because even the most undesirable and tragic events contain the seed for an even greater comeback.

Amor Fati isn't about hopelessly accepting our misfortunes—that's lazy and weak. Instead, it's about *loving* the so-called "bad" things that happen to us—and using that as fuel for a powerful reversal. We shouldn't wish for anything else except what ultimately happens. Love nothing but reality.

> *"Never complain. To complain*
> *always brings discredit.*
> *Better be a model of self-reliance*
> *opposed to the passion of others*
> *than an object of their compassion."*
> **- Baltasar Gracian**

Remember that the Universal Law of life is growth. Therefore, everything that happens within the Universe must be a cause or effect of expansion.

Wallace Wattles wrote in The Science of Getting Rich: *"Every living thing must continually seek for the enlargement of its life, because life, in the mere act of living, must increase itself. A seed, dropped*

into the ground, springs into activity, and in the act
of living produces a hundred more seeds; life, by
living, multiplies itself. It is forever becoming more;
it must do so, if it continues to be at all."

The Universe is a living thing; therefore,
everything that happens within its boundaries must
also align with its nature. And, as Mr. Wattles said,
its nature is increase. This provides us with a more
resilient system of judgment than the mushy
measure of good versus evil. The Few and Insurgents
should base their actions on whether they're in line
with the increase that the Universe demands—and
thereby being desirable—or if they're stunting
growth and, therefore, undesirable.

This takes us back to Nietzche's concept of
Master-slave morality. He explained that for strong-
willed persons, the "good" is the noble, strong, and
powerful, while the "bad" is the weak, cowardly,
timid, and petty. The "good" is always value-creating
for the group, and what is "bad" is harmful to the
system as a whole.

Strong, value-creating actions not only earn us
the mental and financial freedom we're seeking, they
also help us achieve a form of spiritual freedom. If
we're taking steps that promote growth for everyone

around us, we too, will benefit from the rising tide we helped build. We are essentially sowing good Karma for ourselves, and that's also what we will reap. If you put out something undesirable, the undesirable comes back to you sooner or later. This is the noblest measure of your actions. This is an intense acceptance of reality.

Approach any hardship with courage and enthusiasm. If your path demands you to walk through hell, walk as if you own the place.

Premeditatio Malorum

The ancient Stoics would perform a powerful exercise: Premeditatio Malorum (premeditation of evils). They would visualize the worst-case outcome of any action before taking it. Doing this would induce the anguish and fear of tragedy in advance. This way, if the worst happens (which it rarely does), the emotions feel less shocking in the moment.

This acts like a vaccine. You've given yourself a dose of the harm ahead of time. So when an undesirable scenario shows up, your body has practiced how to react.

As Seneca once wrote to a friend, "Nothing happens to the wise man against his expectation, . . . nor do all things turn out for him as he wished but as he reckoned—and above all, he reckoned that something could block his plans."

Locus of Control: Proximity Is Leverage

The closer something is to us, the more power over it we can have. This means our inner world—our mind—is the thing we have the most control over. If you control your inner monologue, you'll enjoy self-control and, therefore, have power over yourself.

If you can't control your own mind, you can't control anything. You become just a feather in the wind.

As we radiate out from our inner selves, we gradually lose some capacity for leverage. It causes diminishing returns. If you can't control your mind, how can you control your household? If you can't control your household, how can you hope to influence your community? And if you can't influence your community, how can you effect change in your city?

Proximity is leverage.

Technically, we can't control what happens to us; we can only really control how we react. It's not about the cards you're dealt but how you play them.

Life is unpredictable, and that's what makes it tough. The sooner you can internalize this lesson, the sooner you can start enjoying your life.

"Planning is important,
but the most important part
of every plan is to plan on the plan
not going according to plan."
- Morgan Housel in The Psychology of
Money

If you want external rewards, remember the proper order of things. It's *Be, Do, Have*. First, you must *Be* the type of person who would have those things, then *Do* the things that flow naturally from being this type of person, and finally, you will *Have* the things such a person has.

Once you become a better *you*, everything you do becomes better. And doing better translates into having better.

If you want wealth, power, or glory, you must first plant the seeds for it internally. This way, you can't help but do what a wealthy person does. And eventually, you will have wealth.

Don't forget the order, and don't skip steps. Or you'll short-circuit the process. This explains why most lottery winners eventually end up broke. They were given all this money without first having the consciousness of a rich person. Lacking this, they don't do the things a rich person does, and the money soon goes.

But when you optimize the things which are closest, you now have a fair shot at success. Proximity is leverage, so start with the immediate. From the inside out. It begins with two things: your thoughts and this moment. Control your thoughts at this moment. The past is gone, and the future isn't here yet. The best way to obtain a good future outcome is to work hard on it right now.

"We can make a little order where we are,
and then the big sweep of history
on which we can have no effect
doesn't overwhelm us.
We do it with colors, with a garden,

with the furnishings of a room,
or with sounds and words.
We make a little form,
and we gain composure."
- Robert Frost

The Happiness Formula

Tom Magliozzi is credited with one of my favorite quotes. He said, "Happiness equals reality minus expectations." More than just a quote, it's the formula to optimize your life.

Let's write it in mathematical terms:
Happiness = Reality - Expectations

Reality is the starting point for all happiness. If your prior expectations are higher than your current reality, all your internal joy is wiped away. Give it a try with actual numbers. If let's say, your reality right now is a 7, but your previous expectations were at level 9, then 7 minus 9 equals -2. You would find yourself very unhappy since your value of happiness turns out to be negative.

Now try different numbers. If your current reality is a 7, but your expectations were only a 3, your happiness level is a 4. It's positive.

In the second example, you're much happier since your happiness went from a -2 to a 4. But your reality didn't change, only the expectations you held beforehand.

Your suffering is merely a disconnect from reality. Wouldn't it be better to set your expectations to virtually 0? Or even negative? Then you'd always be happy.

I turn to negative visualization when I feel too excited about what's coming. For example, if I were visiting a theme park with friends tomorrow, I'd spend a couple of minutes today thinking about what could go wrong. Maybe the weather will turn stormy and the rides close. Or perhaps the lines are extra long. Or maybe the car breaks down on the way there. Life is unpredictable; anything can happen. Simply thinking about possible mishaps tames my expectations. If a great time isn't guaranteed, even a good time will suffice.

The formula checks out. Our expectations determine our mood and contentment. You should aim to be as rooted in reality as possible and limit how much you fantasize. You can only do this by gaining a real feel for life through experimentation. Through rejecting the illusions of the Fog and following your gut instincts.

To be clear, I don't espouse becoming a depressed ogre with no goals who thinks life sucks. Quite the opposite: I want you to set high standards for yourself. To place a high value on what you bring to the table and to desire big things. But these high standards must be backed up with equally massive action. The action grounds you in reality while limiting your fantasies.

We have it all backward. Most of us have low standards and high expectations. Instead, happiness comes from having high standards in the moment but low expectations for the future. I demand the best in the present but expect the worst in the future. This way, my expectations never overshadow my reality.

Buddhists espouse the *Middle Way*, meaning they prefer to live in moderation and avoid extremes.

Our fantasies about the future come from our desires. Merely thinking of what we want produces a chemical response in the brain, which brings pleasure. If left unchecked, we become addicted to fantasizing about our goals while not really doing anything to get closer to those goals.

Massive desires require massive action.

The same thing applies to our fears. If we have a goal but fear of failure prevents us from pursuing the goal, then we've also fallen out of sync with reality. The antidote to both these extreme emotions is action. Action is the middle path that grounds us in reality. We get closer to reality only by taking action since now we see the price of our dreams. Paying that price—the action towards realization—liberates us from the Fog.

Between desire and fear, there is action. Action allows us to *feel* reality instead of merely fantasizing about a rosy future. Action links us to our Rich Instinct.

We've already discussed the benefits of visualizing all the worst things that could happen. Seneca said that nothing happens to the wise man contrary to his expectation because he has considered every possibility—even the cruel and heartbreaking ones.

"Peace begins where expectation ends."
- Sri Chinmoy

The same principle applies to interpersonal dynamics. Expect nothing from others.

We suffer when we put our beliefs in anything but reality. Especially when we put our belief in other humans, collectively or individually. Everyone is living their own movie in their head. So how can you expect your values to match the values of those around you?

Reality is the only thing we should be holding onto for support. Life is much freer that way. It weighs less, and therefore the stumbles hurt much less too.

Much of our suffering comes from thinking transactionally: giving in order to get. The implicit promise is, "I will do this nice thing for you, and I expect you will perform a similar nice gesture in return." That's a recipe for disappointment. Everyone has their own love language, so your nice gesture could go unnoticed. Or could even be perceived as an insult, prompting retaliation. Alternatively, they might return your gift in a love language that doesn't register with you. You're out of sync with each other.

Love and friendship must be a natural outpouring of giving, not a quid-pro-quo. It can't be forced. Give only what you want to give, for no other reason than it pleases you to give this way. The self-fulfillment of being generous might be the only reward you ever receive; therefore, it's the only thing you should expect to get. If the other person happens to return your kind treatment in a pleasing way, let that be merely icing on the cake.

Although it sounds callous and detached, the best strategy is to imagine no one cares about you. With that, also imagine no one is intentionally trying to hurt you. In reality, everyone is too busy thinking about themselves; their actions towards you are just a byproduct of their journey.

Everything you need is already inside of you. You have abundant gifts to offer the world and should use your talents to help your community. But don't expect your community to take care of you. If they do, great. But you must give for the love of giving without expecting rewards.

As Steven Pressfield said of the Bhagavad Gita: "Krishna instructed Arjuna: "We have a right to our labor, but not to the fruits of our labor." What did he mean by that? He meant that the process is its own reward. The only real reward." Well, we also have a right to give love, but not to receive love. In time, The Universe will repay you according to how much love and value you give; you just won't see it coming. But it'll be *more* than worth it.

"Free your mind of the idea of deserving,
of the idea of earning,
and you will begin to be able to think."
- Ursula K. Le Guin in The Dispossessed

A Reality Free of Attachment

During our darkest moments, we tend to ask ourselves, "Why has The Universe done this to me?" The pain sometimes comes from a new burden we must carry, but more often, it comes from losing something. During those times, it helps to recall Marcus Aurelius' wise words, "Loss is nothing else but change, and change is nature's delight."

Change is the driving force behind all growth. Without change, nothing grows. And remember, the Universal Law of life is growth. When things stop growing, they start dying. If you want to stay in the good graces of God or The Universe, you must also align yourself with growth.

If you're tuned into The Universe, you'll realize all the changes happening around you are simply growth taking effect. Everything that happens—desirable or undesirable—is simply data on the growth process. Information about the true nature of reality. Wishing things were different is wishing for ignorance.

In your quest to get closer to reality, don't run away from problems. And don't be attached to the status quo. Growth requires tension, just as you would lift weights to make your muscles grow. The greater the resistance, the bigger the growth.

Instinctively, our mind and body crave tension. They crave resistance. Otherwise, why would you feel so good after pushing yourself during a hard run? The "runner's high" is your body finally getting the stress it longed for. An absence of problems isn't just undesirable; it would actually prevent you from experiencing happiness. The tension created from struggle is the source of joy.

As part of this living organism called Earth, we're all on this journey toward growth, whether we want to be or not. Only when we die can we get off this train. In the meantime, rid yourself of attachment to how things used to be. Nostalgia and romanticizing "the good ol' days" are toxic for growth.

Your mind will find whatever it looks for. If you look for things to be depressed about, you will find them. But if you look for things to be happy about, you will find plenty of that too. Happiness is simply a choice. A choice that must be made again and again at every moment, or depression will take hold.

Life is wild. Or, as many philosophers have labeled it: life is absurd. Just when we think we've seen it all, life shows us something new. Life isn't normal with fleeting moments of absurdity; it's absurd with a smoke screen of normalcy. This smoke screen is the Fog.

Alan Watts taught us to live free from attachment to the past. According to him, true certainty and security come only from understanding that impermanence and insecurity are the essence of our existence. Accepting uncertainty is liberating. Only then are we truly free to move with The Universe. Toni Morrison wrote, "If you surrendered to the air, you could ride it."

Live in the moment. And live as close to reality as you can. Avoid attachment to the past or the future. Neither of those is real. Only this moment is real. Life is made up of present time and presence of mind.

> *"Live your life as if you are ready to*
> *say goodbye to it at any moment,*
> *as if the time left for you were*
> *some pleasant surprise."*
> **- Marcus Aurelius**

Chapter 10:
DO LESS TO ACCOMPLISH MORE: THE SUPERPOWER OF BEING RELAXED

Marcus Aurelius, one of Rome's greatest emperors, said, "The greatest part of what we say and do is really unnecessary. If a man takes this to heart, he will have more leisure and less uneasiness." This humble quote has a boatload of supporting mathematics beneath the surface.

In 1906, the Italian economist Vilfredo Pareto made a bold claim. He said that 20% of inputs are responsible for about 80% of results. Regarding business, 80% of sales usually come from just the top 20% of a company's products. Likewise, 80% of profits typically come from the top 20% of customers.

In more practical applications, if you carpet your house, you'll notice that around 80% of the traffic travels on just 20% of the surface area of the carpet. At the same time, the remaining 80% of the carpet's area gets minimal action. Meaning the popular—and effective—inputs of any activity are what will produce the vast majority of the outcomes. This 80% to 20% ratio is why they call it the 80/20 principle.

It lines up nicely with what Marcus Aurelius said. The greatest part of what we do is actually unnecessary. Therefore, a wise person should always look for the "necessary" actions and focus their energy there first.

"What the pupil must learn,
if he learns anything,
is that the world will do most
of the work for you,
provided you cooperate with
it by identifying
how it really works
and aligning with those realities."
- Joseph Tussman

The caveat here is that parsing the necessary from the unnecessary often takes *a lot* of work at first. We'll have to try many things and consider them mini-experiments towards a goal.

But it all starts with the realization that your greatest triumphs come from just a few powerful moves.

We should all be like the great Marcus Aurelius. Realizing that most of our actions don't produce results, we can cut out the unproductive things we do, and our days would have much more peace. Or, if our aim is to attain more—such as financial independence—then we can do more of the productive stuff to create *more* money in less time.

Gary Keller runs the biggest real estate brokerage in the world. In his early days, he noticed company growth was slowing, yet he was working harder than ever. Then he discovered the issue. He was spreading himself thin with tasks of secondary importance. That's when he developed "The One Thing." He started asking himself, "What is the one thing I can do now that will make everything else easier or unnecessary?" The answer he got: he was working more when he needed to delegate more. He then focused on finding the best department heads he could find. Once he had all-stars running each group, company growth skyrocketed, and his life became a breeze.

If you chase two rabbits, you will not catch either one.

It sounds too obvious, but success is a matter of focus. Your energy should first go toward the one thing that will produce the most results. Once that's taken care of, there will be a next "one thing" that should be tackled first.

The "less is more" approach also applies to your relationships. Focus first on those who already value who you are, because you already have leverage with them. This will produce more results with less effort since they like you, admire you, and want to help you. Minimal arm twisting is needed with your loyal supporters. As Seth Godin once told me, "It makes more sense to engage with people who want to hear from you than yelling at people who are trying to ignore you." In business, the term they use for this is "product-market fit." A company that is aligned with a receptive market will quickly succeed. If what you have is water, find those who are thirsty.

Like all other concepts, this extreme focus on the essential requires major courage. It's not for the weak. The things you choose to ignore will still beckon for your attention. The unproductive relationships you de-prioritize will sling guilt trips your way. You will miss some birthday parties and weddings that conflict with your goals. Your job is to stay strong and keep your chosen course. You will focus on the essential and only tend to the less important once the first-rate items have been taken care of.

The rewards of this streamlined approach soon start to compound. Since you're doing a smaller variety of things, you also become *better* at these things. You're a specialist in this narrower market. You become faster, and your reputation increases. Now you're worth more at these activities. You will be rewarded with stronger bonds, higher wages, and more enjoyment. Your life has shifted to a higher plane.

Don't just think of it as "less is more." Think of it as "less but better."

Aside from the rewards of specialization, there are tons more rewards to be enjoyed from doing less. You have more white space in your schedule when you do fewer things. You can now go about your day without feeling rushed. This means you are in total control of your wits, and you are acting in a relaxed manner.

To clarify, doing less doesn't mean being lazy or renouncing striving. Quite the opposite, it means going all-in on fewer—but more important—things. Do less things, yet do them with more intensity and focus. Again, less but better.

Within the few essential disciplines you dedicate yourself to, you can now do more and experiment more. You're driven and hungry but never in a panicked rush. Since you've reduced the number of things you do, you have more time for the critical few things and more time between tasks to relax and recharge. Even if you decide to work long hours on your priorities, this is a decision you made, and you're still free because you own your time. Choice is freedom.

Throughout a career that spans five decades, Bill Murray has learned a thing or two. My favorite advice from him came during a New York Times interview where he said, "The more relaxed you are, the better you are at everything: the better you are with your loved ones, the better you are with your enemies, the better you are at your job, the better you are with yourself." He also said, "That's sort of why I got into acting. I realized the more fun I had, the better I did it."

Notice how there are no conditions in his statement. In everything you do, being relaxed will always lead to better results than panicking. Not worrying allows you to have fun and learn quicker. When you're relaxed, you free up mental and physical resources that can be re-directed to the task at hand.

Desperation Debilitates and Destroys

One of the quickest ways to drift into the Fog is through panic or desperation. Once again, Marcus Aurelius understood this well. He once wrote in his journal, "The nearer a man comes to a calm mind, the closer he is to strength."

A calm mind is powerful because it gives us the luxury of a broader perspective. It creates mental space. We see more of the landscape, and due to this, more options to maneuver around situations. But when we panic, our heart races, pushing our reactionary glands into overdrive. Our body turns on the "Fight or Flight" switch, which hyper-focuses us on whatever danger is in front of us. This helped our ancestors survive in the wild. But we no longer live in the wild, so the Fight or Flight mode becomes less useful. Fight or Flight brings tunnel vision, cutting off valuable information from the periphery. The picture in our eyes becomes small and flat so that we can see the granular details needed for escape. Tunnel vision shows us options A and B, but a calm mind shows us A through Z.

Worrying doesn't help; it steals your power.

Our enemies will use worry against us. They will plant booby traps to divert our attention. If we get distracted, we will soon find ourselves on a fool's errand, neglecting meaningful action in favor of fake urgency.

A Relaxed Demeanor Yields More Leverage

Remember: the more relaxed you are, the better you are at everything. It pays dividends internally and externally.

As mentioned above, being relaxed benefits your internal process.

But serenity also brings more help from the outside. See, as humans, we're all attracted to growth and prosperity. Growth and prosperity mean surplus. An excess of resources. You have more money than you need, more strength than your tasks require, and more time than you've promised away. These are all instances of surplus. Well, it turns out the best way to indicate abundance is to be relaxed. A relaxed demeanor signals you're far from your limits. It communicates, "My resources run deep; I'm nowhere close to my max." We flock to that. Derek Sivers advised entrepreneurs to "Set up your business like you don't need the money, and it'll likely come your way."

Here's the best way to get a bank to loan you money: show them that you don't need the loan. Good businessfolk work hard to sculpt their application and make it seem like they don't need the money. This is a delicate balance of showing the bank your numbers in a positive light and a nonchalance about needing the money to begin with. Not desperate, just "eh, whatever."

Daniel Ally says money hates desperate people. And anyone who works desperately for money will have none of it. The same goes for everything. Others get turned off by desperation.

But composure is sexy.

> *"I always started a job with the feeling*
> *that I'd soon quit or be fired,*
> *and this gave me a relaxed manner that*
> *was mistaken for intelligence*
> *or some secret power."*
> **- Charles Bukowski**

This type of aura is irresistible to others. It's a magnet for assistance and attention. It's the essence of "charisma" and the famous "it factor." When you're relaxed, you benefit from more than just your energy; you also have others propelling you forward. All the roadblocks magically disappear.

The Tide of Life

Nature, as we all know, has its seasons and moods. Energy concentrates at one place today and another tomorrow. Like a pendulum, what today is up, tomorrow will be down. A rising tide lifts all boats. When things are in season or a fad kicks in, everyone associated with it automatically gets a boost. You don't have to be exceptionally talented during these high tides to thrive. All you need is to be in the game.

Someone astute—as you now are—just needs to observe where the tide is going and learn how to roll with it. Look where money is moving and stand in the way.

Ryan Holiday wrote about another of Marcus Aurelius' observations this way:

"The best stuff in life is an accidental byproduct. Marcus Aurelius marvels at "nature's inadvertence." A baker, he writes, makes the dough, kneads it and then puts it in the oven. Then physics, then Nature takes over. "The way loaves of bread split open," Marcus writes, "the ridges are just byproducts of the baking, and yet pleasing, somehow: they rouse our appetite without our knowing why."

The same goes for life. Most of our rewards will be accidental byproducts of our mere presence. Those who love you most, love you simply because you're you. What you are—and what you stand for—naturally attracts them. This is why a great friendship seems effortless. You already have their attention and support for just *being you.* The moment you start trying too hard, the chemistry changes.

"Nature does not hurry,
but everything is accomplished."
- Lao Tzu

The highest rewards in life come not from the exhausting effort you put in but from simply finding those who *already* value what you bring to the table. Those who truly appreciate you will provide more help, encouraging words, love, and monetary support than those you chase. Simply find those who already value what you have. Once you implement this, doing less will bring you more. More of what you value. More abundance, in every sense of the word.

CHAPTER 11:
BE UNSTOPPABLE: THE
ART OF MOMENTUM

Nature is abundant and undefeated because it's always moving, always adapting. As long as it continues to do so, it will survive and thrive. In this way, even a misstep is still a step.

Take a page out of nature's playbook. You will sometimes make mistakes in your quest for mental and financial freedom. So realize it's part of the game you've chosen. You are the gladiator in the arena taking blows, not the timid spectator in the stands.

As they say in military circles, "no battle plan survives first contact with the enemy." You don't know what you don't know until you start. This is why we've said the solutions never make sense ahead of time; otherwise, the problem would've been solved long ago. When you start making moves, reality will show you all the mistakes in your plan.

And some of these mistakes will feel like the world is ending. At first glance, you will see no way out. You will be in panic mode. But I want you to know one thing: there is always a way through. The great ones eventually learn that a mistake made with boldness can be corrected with more boldness. Muhammad Ali explained this when he used boxing as a metaphor for life. He said, "You don't lose if you get knocked down; you lose if you stay down."

In your quest out of the Fog, you, too, must live by Ali's philosophy: it's ok to hit the mat occasionally, but it's not ok to stay on the mat. Get up and keep fighting.

"I was fighting a small fight of my own which
wasn't leading anywhere --
but like a man with a bent spoon trying
to dig through a cement wall
I knew that a small fight was better than quitting:
it kept the heart alive."
- Charles Bukowski

Life is an endless series of problems. You'll solve one problem, and a new problem will soon arise. Often, the solution to the original problem is what brings on the next problem. Problems never stop; they merely get exchanged and/or upgraded. Happiness comes from solving problems. Don't waste time wondering why life has such a twisted sense of humor; just keep moving and work on the following problem. You can't stop the waves, but you can learn how to surf.

Problems never stop. Neither should you.

"The only way to make sense out of change
is to plunge into it,
move with it, and join the dance."
- Alan Watts

I like the analogy of life as a game of chess. When you're in a tight spot, and your king is in danger, it's useless to wish for the rules to be different. You can't change the rules of this game we call life. The chess board is the chess board. The only thing left to do is make the best move available to you at each moment. You get out of trouble the same way you got into trouble: move by move, step by step.

*"There are two types of people in this world:
those who resist change
in favor of nostalgia
and those who move with the times
and create a better future."*
- Phil M Jones in Exactly What to Say

If you're like me, most of your suffering comes from overthinking. I'll try to think myself out of a problem when in reality, solutions only come through action. When you stop thinking and start moving, the way appears. You don't have to get it right; you just have to get it going. Through your Rich Instinct and your sense of feeling, you will find the next step that leads to the step after that. Before you know it, the obstacle is way back there.

The tech world has a concept termed "MVP." It stands for Minimum Viable Product. As in, "What's the simplest, cheapest version of my idea that I can test in public?"

In 1999, the founder of Zappos had the idea to sell shoes online. But he wasn't sure if it would work. Instead of spending years—and millions of dollars—building his grand vision, he made a simple website with photos of the shoes he wanted to sell. And he bought no inventory. When he got an order, he'd run to a store and buy that shoe, then ship it out. He saw immediate success and then scaled up gradually. Amazon eventually bought Zappos for $1.2 Billion.

The concept is simple: make your next move your best move. Every powerful action relies on timing, so there's no sense in saving your best move for later. It might not work later. If its time is now, use it now.

Repeat this enough, and soon you'll create the habit of putting your best foot forward at each moment. You create a groove. It becomes second nature, and you do precisely what the moment calls for. Be fluid, like water, and nothing can stop you.

The world will often look chaotic, but instead of fighting it, embrace it.

"Let go and move with the chaos that presents itself to you—from within it,
you will find endless opportunities
that elude most people.
Don't give others the chance to pin you down;
keep moving and changing your appearances
to fit the environment.

If you encounter walls or boundaries,
slip around them.
Do not let anything disrupt your flow."
- Robert Greene in The 50th Law

When you keep moving, never stopping for too long, you learn much faster than those around you. You develop a connection with the world's ways— and with humans around you. And this connection cuts through the illusions that cloud the vision of others. This connection keeps you far from the Fog.

Remember: Life is change. Life is movement. There's no set-it-and-forget-it button. You must constantly balance and counter-balance, or perish.

If you've been feeling your way through this world, then you've been honing your Rich Instinct. It will serve you right, and you will be unstoppable because you are in tune with The Universe. In tune with change. In tune with growth. Just. Keep. Moving.

"People wish to be settled;
only as far as they are unsettled
is there any hope for them."
- Ralph Waldo Emerson

ACKNOWLEDGEMENTS

Big thank you to my parents, Cecilia and Ramon. You two show me daily what it's like to be a generous and fearless human in this complicated world.

Thank you Rocio and Randy for accepting me just as I am, and for your full support in everything I do. It means more to me than you'll ever know.

Thank you Moises, Melanie, Natalie, Sophia, Miguelina, and Lucas. I feel privileged to call you family. I learn something from each of you daily.

To my crew: Dre, Ardy, Chris, Analin, Madeline, and Andreina. Thank you for helping me grow into a much better person. Your diverse perspectives are a big inspiration for this book. The book wouldn't exist without you.

Major thank you to my dear friend and mentor, Al Pittampalli. You were the only person who even knew I was writing this book. There's no way I could've persevered without your encouraging words and advice. I'm extremely grateful for your counsel and feedback on the content. I owe you big time.

Thank you Melissa for quickly becoming such a nurturing and supportive presence in my life. You get me in a way that very few do.

Thank you Robert Greene for being a mentor from afar. Your books and way of thinking opened up a whole new world inside my mind.

There are still many more of you who were a major influence in my life and this piece of work. I thank you from the bottom of my heart. Let's continue being a positive force in this world.

SELECTED BIBLIOGRAPHY

Aurelius, Marcus. Meditations – Gregory Hays translation

Clear, James. Atomic Habits

Coelho, Paulo. The Alchemist

Cole-Whitaker, Terry. What You Think of Me Is None Of My Business

Gracian, Baltasar. The Art of Worldly Wisdom

Greene, Robert. - The 48 Laws of Power - The 50th Law - Mastery

Holiday, Ryan. - The Obstacle Is The Way - Courage is Calling

Housel, Morgan. The Psychology of Money

Keller, Gary and Papasan, Jay. The One Thing

Kishimi, Ichiro and Koga, Fumitake. The Courage to be Disliked

Machiavelli, Niccolo. The Prince

Manson, Mark. The Subtle Art of Not Giving a F*ck

Plato. The Republic

Pressfield, Steven. The War of Art

Ries, Al. The 22 Immutable Laws of Marketing

Ruiz, Don Miguel. The Four Agreements

Wachowskis. The Matrix

Wattles, Wallace. The Science of Getting Rich

ABOUT THE AUTHOR

ALEX CESPEDES is a business consultant specializing in capital advisory and marketing. He's been contracted by industry-leading companies like Morgan Stanley, Muscle Milk, and 5-Hour Energy. A long-time podcaster, he spends his days gathering and sharing the best knowledge on how to thrive as an entrepreneur in today's fast-paced market. Find out more at AlexCespedes.com

Made in United States
North Haven, CT
23 August 2023

40685801R00129